Salvation and Wholeness

THE BIBLICAL PERSPECTIVES OF HEALING

by John P. Baker

Fountain Trust
London

Printed in England by
Green & Co. (Lowestoft) Ltd.
Crown Street, Lowestoft

Preface

This book began as a paper read at Tyndale House, Cambridge, in July 1972, at a meeting of the Biblical Theology study group of the Tyndale Fellowship for Biblical Research, of which group the author is the secretary. The general theme of the group's studies that year was "Man in renewal", and the paper on "Wholeness and salvation" was only one of the six papers read under that general theme. Encouraged by the lively discussion that followed and by the advice of friends afterwards, the writer decided to prepare the paper for publication. It is now over double its original length, having been expanded to try and cover the ten major points raised in the discussion, and two other matters. One or two of these are covered in appendices, so that the general flow of the argument should not be held up by them. All footnotes to both the text and appendices will be found at the end of the book. However, this work does not represent any official policy or teaching of the Tyndale Fellowship, and the author accepts sole and entire responsibility for it.

The author wishes to thank all those who contributed to the discussion in Cambridge, and especially those who encouraged him to seek publication for this material, the Revd. Dr. Jim Packer (Chairman of the study group), the Revd. Derek Kidner (Warden of Tyndale House), the Revd. C. N. Hillyer (Librarian of Tyndale House), and the Revd. Dr. Colin Brown, who gave the Tyndale Biblical Theology Lecture that year. He also thanks Miss Joyce Gardner who typed the manuscript twice in preparation for Cambridge and for publication.

This exposition is offered to the Lord's people with the earnest prayer that it may be used by Him to raise the level of faith in His promises of healing, and to enable the church of Christ to see this subject in its true biblical perspective, so that the Name of our Lord Jesus Christ, the only Saviour and the great Physician, may be glorified more abundantly in the eyes of men, as they continue to see and extol more of the wonderful works of our almighty and gracious God.

John P. Baker

This book is
dedicated to my wife ALISON
whose constant love, faith and
encouragement have brought to me
and to many others so much more of the
wholeness of God's great salvation in Jesus our Lord.

Contents

Introduction

Aims and Perspectives

In view of the vastness of this subject, which touches nearly all of the great themes of the Bible in both Testaments, and on which such a great number of books have been written in this century, this study will be no more than an introductory survey of the biblical material on it. The aim is to set the whole idea of healing in the Bible in the context of the Bible's view of man, life, death, salvation, redemption and the progress of the Kingdom of God, and in the light of that to attempt to correlate the biblical view of healing into some sort of positive and coherent whole. We are not here concerned with the history of the subject in the Christian church, nor with discussing individual cases either of "success" or "failure" (so-called), for two reasons: first, that in this study we are concerned with biblical theology, and also that in the present writer's judgment that would be an error in method, which would lead us to try to fit the word of God to, and to test it by, our experience and its paucity, rather than to test our experience by the word of God and its inexhaustible riches.

1. Man in death and life

Man According to the Bible

The one thing about which every study of the Scriptural doctrine of man in the last few decades agrees, is that man, God's creature made in His own image, is an indivisible unity; if you prefer it, a psycho-physical unity — one person. For the purposes of study, analysis, and clear thought we may in speech isolate different aspects of the one person or life, physical, mental, emotional, volitional, spiritual etc.; but as G. C. Berkouwer[1] points out, we could never derive any such neat and methodical compartmentalizing of man from the biblical account of him, whether you view that account in terms of theology, anthropology, psychology or sociology. Much has been written on this, and on the contrast between the Hebrew and biblical picture of man, and the pagan division of man into body and spirit (whether under the influence of Greek Platonic philosophy or of the oriental pagan religions). We shall not add to it here, except to observe that the domination of Christian thinking by the fragmented pagan theory of man has been responsible as much as anything for over-clouding the biblical perspective of salvation and healing.

Man in Death and Life, or Lostness and Salvation,

(a) *The state of man lost and fallen — "Death"*

According to the Old and New Testaments the state brought about by man's sin and disobedience is fundamentally one of alienation from God under His judgement (or "wrath"). As a result of that judgment, and of man's violation of his own nature as utterly dependent on his Creator for life in His image, man became a subjected slave under the rule of the "tyrants" (as Luther called them) of death, the devil (and his demonic powers), sin, and the law — the dominion or lordship of darkness at every level of his being and at each stage of his existence. This involved the progressive dislocation and disintegration of man, in himself and in all his relationships (Romans chapters 1 to 8 *passim*). By the inner law of the universe and of his own being as a creation of the living God, this meant *death* as the fundamental state and destiny of fallen man — for "All who hate Me, love death" (Prov. 8:36).

With our analytical minds trained in Graeco-Roman logic and thought-forms, we immediately begin to split up this term "death", into something like "spiritual", "physical" and "eternal". But the New Testament does not do this any more than Genesis does. Adam and Eve entered the state of death on the day they ate of the tree, as God had said that they would, although its culmination in their mortal bodies may have been several hundred years in its outworking (Gen. 2:17; 3:19, 24; 5:5; cf. Eph. 2:1ff.). Similarly in Rom. 5: 12ff.; so completely unified is Paul's view of death, that commentators have been able to argue over what aspect of death he was talking about. The "second death" in Revelation 20 is simply the final and eternal ratification, fixation and culmination of the sentence and state of death, in which those who refused life have been from the first. So disease came into the world as part of this enslavement or subjection to death, mortality, corruption, and Satan, that followed the fall of man into sin (Gen. 3; Job 1 & 2; Rom. 5:12ff., 8:2 and intervening passages; Acts 10: 38).

(b) *The state of man in salvation — "Life"*

God's salvation in Christ delivers man from this state, and it does so basically by re-instating man into fellowship and acceptance with God through the vicarious death and resurrection of Jesus Christ. From alienation we move into acceptance, from slavery to the dreaded "tyrants" into sonship of God, from death into life, and from the lordship of darkness into the kingdom or reign of God in Christ (Rom. 6 and 7; 2 Cor. 5:18-21; Col. 1:13-14, 21-22). As Paul puts it: "The law (that is the authoritative declaration, or the announced rule) of the Spirit of life in Christist

Jesus has set us free from the law (i.e. the judicial sentence or rule) of sin and death" (Rom. 8:2). We are now in the sphere of *life* — and here precisely the same complete and unitary view of this life state, of this "eternal life", obtains in the Bible as we observed when thinking about "death".[2] This can be illustrated from the biblical images of life (see Appendix A on *The river of Life etc.*, pp. 55ff.). It is perfectly true that the Greek New Testament has two words (*zōē* and *bios*) to cover our term "life" in general (besides *psuchē*, which describes a "life" in the sense of its being the personal possession and identity of an individual — though it is translated more frequently by other words, notably "soul"). But the distinction between *zōē* and *bios* is not that between spiritual life and physical life, but rather between the life which is properly so-called (life under God and in communion with Him, at all its levels and stages), and life which is not properly so-called (mere existence — actually in a state of "death" according to Scripture — in separation or alienation from God who is Life). While *zōē* is occasionally used in a general indiscriminate sense, *bios* and its cognates are only used of the latter. So the Christian was dead, but is now alive; he was in death, he is now in life. Indeed one might well summarize the good news of the kingdom of God as the reign of grace, life and righteousness through Jesus Christ (Romans chapters 5 to 8, esp. 5: 20-21). We have been transferred from the one kingdom to the other (Col. 1: 12-14). And in the new kingdom, Christ not only reigns over us, but we sit in the heavenlies and conquer and reign with Him (Eph. 2: 5ff.; Rev. chs. 4; 20; *et passim*).

Stages in the coming of the kingdom and the experience of salvation

In the teaching of Christ the kingdom of God comes in at least three stages: the first co-incides with His own person and ministry; the second begins with His exaltation and the outpouring of the Holy Spirit; and the third, the

11

consummation, ensues upon the *parousia*, His personal return in glory at the end. Equally in the individual Christian's, and the church's, experience of salvation, although that salvation is essentially a unity, yet corresponding to the tenses of the verb used (e.g. by Paul and Peter), we can distinguish in principle three stages: we have been saved (Eph. 2: 8) from sin's penalty and alienation; we are being saved (1 Cor. 1: 18) from its power and effects in our lives; we shall be saved (Rom. 5: 10; 1 Pet. 1: 9) from sin's very presence and every vestige of its effects, receiving imperishable spiritual bodies to dwell in a renewed world (Rom. 8: 18-25).

Excursus: the Bodily Death or "Sleep" of the Christian

Immediately, therefore, we become aware of an apparent anomaly, possibly even a flaw, in the account of this salvation from death to life, which we already enjoy in a real way, though not yet in its final stage. We have already passed from death to life (John 5: 24); yet evidently the Christian still dies, physically, to await bodily resurrection at the last day (vv. 28-9). But the New Testament will not even allow us to say that *simpliciter*. The believer, whichever translation of John 11: 25-26 you prefer ("never die" or "not die eternally"), does not "die"; he "falls asleep" in Jesus who is Life (see e.g. John 11:11; 1 Cor. 15:6, 18, 20, 51; 1 Thess. 4:13ff.). The dissolution and separation of his mortal body are an interruption of his waking life, nay more, an anomaly (see 2 Cor. 5: 1-10) — though even this is far better than indefinite continuance in this life and world (Phil. 1:19-26). To what is this anomaly due? The Bible will not allow us to say simply that it is due to our still being under the rule of death, for we are not, although our last enemy is not yet finally abolished and utterly destroyed (1 Cor. 15: 26). The answer would seem to lie along the line of three considerations: (a) the postponement of the day of final judgement of all

12

evil powers and men, to give more men the opportunity to repent (2 Pet. 3: 9-15); (b) the consequent postponement of the renewal of the whole creation, of man's environment — this is the tension of the Christian living in the "coming" or "new" age, and yet without the "old" or "present (evil)" age from which we are saved having finally and entirely passed away (Rom. 8: 18ff.; Gal. 1: 4). This is expounded by Paul in terms of the whole physical creation's bondage to corruption or decay (*phthora*), in which our present mortal "flesh and blood" physical constitutions still appear to share (Rom. 8:18-25); and from which we shall only be finally delivered when we receive our resurrection bodies at the last day, and the whole of the physical order is finally renewed *aphthartos* (imperishable), or in *aphtharsia* (incorruption) (cf. 1 Cor. 15: 50-54). Therefore the apostle can speak on one occasion of our outward man as "thoroughly perishing" (*diaphtheirein*) in contrast to the inward renewal we are constantly experiencing day by day (2 Cor. 4: 16ff.). (c) the continuance or maintenance of the "faith" principle in this world, through which men are saved, and believers are trained and deepened in their walk with God. If believers never fall asleep, this principle would already have given place to "sight" (2 Cor. 5: 7; cf. Heb. 11).

The physical death of the Christian, then, properly called his "falling asleep", could be looked upon in several lights: as a pause in the development of his abundant life in Christ, or as the final putting off of this mortal or corruptible body, the last trace of the "old man" or first Adam preparatory to receiving the new and glorious resurrection body of the "new man" after the image of the second Man, the last Adam, who is Jesus Christ (see 1 Cor. 15: 45-49). Of this certain and final outworking of the victory over our last enemy, we are given several assuring evidences and tokens in Scripture, including the resurrection of Jesus Christ as the basic guarantee (1 Cor. 15: 22ff.; 2 Cor. 4: 14), and the gift of His renewing Holy Spirit to us now as the "earnest" or "firstfruits" (Rom. 8:23; 2 Cor. 1:22; Eph.

1:13-14); also the temporary raising of not a few other dead (at least eight named individuals, all or most of whom died before a normal length of life had been lived out); the assumption or translation of Enoch and Elijah (Gen. 5:24; Heb. 11:5; 2 Kings 2:11); the appearance of Moses and Elijah on the mountain at the transfiguration (Matt. 17:3 and parallels); and the example of men like Moses, whose death at 120 years old seems not to have been so much the outworking of any law of corruption and death in him, as God withdrawing or receiving his spirit from his body when the number of his days was fulfilled. For he climbed a mountain to die, "his eye was not dim, nor had his natural strength diminished" (Deut. 34: 7), and but for his disobedience at Meribah he would have lived on longer. One cannot but feel that in general, apart from persecution, war etc., this is God's intention for those who have consistently let the Spirit of life in Christ Jesus set them free from the law of sin and death at every level of their being: namely that, at the end of a long and full life ("old and full of days") and in good health, they should breathe their last yielding up their spirit to their Maker when He sees that the number of their days (normally 70-80 years now) are fulfilled, for their times are in His hand (see Gen. 25:8; 35:29; 49:33; Exod. 23:26; Job 42:17; Pss. 31:15; 90:10; 104:29; Eccl. 12:7). (See further Appendix B, page 59ff. on this point.) Of course the phrase "apart from persecution, war, etc." is a big proviso, for the Christian who has suffered torture and martyrdom has not got a second best, since *the best* is yet to come (Rev. 2:10).

We have spent this time on the Christian's physical "falling asleep", because it forms part of the whole subject and appears to be a stumbling-block to some people, which prevents them from taking a positive attitude regarding God's promises about healing; it is hoped that we have said enough to allay such doubts and fears.

The Place of Healing and Wholeness in Salvation from Death to Life

The question that now faces us is this: what is the place of healing and wholeness within the second phase of the coming or progress of the kingdom of God, and within the second stage of the Christian's (and the church's) experience of salvation? Please notice that we did not say "the healing of the *body*", for the simple reason that the Bible does not encourage us to speak in that way. It speaks of the healing of *people*, sick people and sinful people, but people, men and women, not just bodies. It may speak of the life of Jesus being manifest in our bodies (2 Cor. 4: 10-11), or of His Holy Spirit quickening our mortal bodies (not apparently the immortal resurrection ones, by the way — Rom. 8: 11),[3] but this is not the body in disjunction from, or contradistinction to, the person, but *as* the person and as the vehicle of the person's expression and life. (See J. A. T. Robinson in *The Body* (S.C.M. 1952) on *sarx* and *sōma*). A lot of our difficulties and confusion about physical healing derive precisely from the fact that we have isolated it in this quite unbiblical way, either in order to deny it, or in order to affirm it as a separate "thing".

This can be seen very easily in the two extreme and opposing views on this subject prevailing in the Church up to the present time. On the one hand you have those who will simply reel off God's promises on healing and exhort you merely to "believe" and your body will be healed, especially if you have first accepted "salvation" from Christ.[4] Without doubt there are many testimonies of remarkable healings under a ministry like that of T. L. Osborn, but there are also bound to be spiritual tragedies left in the wake of such teaching as well, because you have these two things labelled "healing" and "salvation" wrapped up in two separate parcels. On the other hand Michael Green in his otherwise excellent book *The Meaning of Salvation*[5] succeeds to his own satisfaction in excluding healing from the Gospel today by a double device: first, by asserting that healing is really only a physical picture or "sign" of spiritual and eternal salvation; and secondly, by asserting that any physical healings were associated with the ministry of Jesus Christ in the flesh, and should therefore not be expected to continue. In fact, besides contradicting himself at several points, he is surely just as false to the Scriptures as the first group of people.

In the Bible forgiveness, healing, eternal life, and deliverance from evil etc. are not separate things or parcels, they are all part and parcel of the one salvation of God in Jesus Christ for His people in the Covenant of grace. "Salvation" and "healing" are virtually interchangeable terms. "Save" is used to mean "heal" (in *our* language) and vice-versa. The words "cure" and "heal" are used concerning exorcism and deliverance from evil, and of salvation (see Jer. 3:22; Hos. 5:13; Matt. 13:15; 17:16-18; Luke 4:18; 6:18; 8:2; 9:42; Acts 10:38; 28:27); the word "save" (*sōzō*) is used of healing (see Matt. 9:21-22; Mark 5:23, 28 and 34; 6:56; 10:52; Luke 7:50; 8:48-50; 17:19; Acts 4:9-12; 14:9). The activity and the promises of God regarding healing extend from Genesis to Revelation (e.g. Gen. 20:17; Rev. 22:2).

But equally the terms for healing are not restricted to the healing of the *individual*, any more than merely to the healing of the body. The Bible speaks of the healing of the people, of their diseases, of their broken hearts, of their backslidings, of relationships, of society, even of the land and its waters, and finally of the nations (Pss. 60:2; 103:3; 147:3; 2 Kings 2:21; 2 Chron. 7:14; 30:20; Hos. 14:4; Rev. 22:2). With the possible exception of the last one, all the references are to this present life and not to the hereafter or the new heavens and earth. This is what salvation is all about, God making people whole and restoring human life and society to normality in Jesus Christ. Therefore as we list and think about the detailed evidence, although we may like to focus on the healing of the body or of the individual, we must keep the biblical perspective in

16

mind all the time, and remember that man is a whole, life is a whole, and salvation is a whole. Perhaps we might re-apply a text: "What God has joined together let no man put asunder!"

Further evidence of the wide view that the Bible takes of the notions of disease, health and wholeness can be found in the use made of the Greek terms *hugiēs* (whole, whole-some, sound, healthy) and its cognate verb *hugiainō*, and also *ischuō* (to be strong, well), as well of the Hebrew equivalents *marpē*, and *tōm* and its cognates. Besides being applied to physical health and healing (as in Matt. 9:12; 12:13; 15:31; John 5:6, 9, 11, 14, 15 etc.), they can be used of speech or the tongue (Prov. 15:4; Tit. 2:8), of teaching or doctrine and faith (1 Tim. 1:10; 6:3; 2 Tim. 1:13; 4:3; Tit. 1:9, 13; 2:1-2), and also of the heart, in the psychological sense (Ps. 119:80; Prov. 14:30). Taking all the words used of healing, health and salvation together, we begin to obtain a notion of "wholeness" as meaning completeness, all-round health and life and strength, en-tailing freedom from evil and its effects at every level of our personal being and in all our relationships. That is the good goal to which God's saving purpose seeks to move us on (Rom. 8:28).

When we seek to define the biblical concept of "whole-ness", therefore, our understanding of it has to be shaped and determined both by what we have customarily regard-ed as the idea of "salvation", and by that of "healing". As far as the individual and the church are concerned, it can be conveniently summarized in the words of Rom. 8:29, as being "conformed to the image of His Son", who is the pattern Man, the new Man, at every level of our being; or as attaining to "the perfect (or complete) man" (Eph. 4:13ff.), that is, true humanity. That wholeness which is God's saving will for us consists first and foremost in conformity to Christ's true manhood in spirit, character, attitudes and action, but also in increasing conformity in body, and in the faculties of mind, body and spirit. If this is to be achieved at all, it will involve the healing of attitudes, emotions, mind, imagination, intellect and understanding, will, affections, relationships, and body.

Within the process by which God our Father makes all things concur for our good so as to increase this conformity to the image of Jesus (Rom. 8: 28-29), there is without doubt a place for suffering, which, when rightly and meekly borne for Christ's sake, will refine the character, strengthen faith, and produce steadfastness — in other words, play its part in producing that wholeness which is God's perfect will for His children (Rom. 5: 3-5; Heb. 12: 5-11; Jas. 1: 2-4; I Pet. 1:6-9; 4:12ff.).[6] Because of this, some Christians assert that disease is to be accepted as part of that perfect will of God, as God's best in this life for some of His children. But this does not necessarily follow at all.[7] What the writers of these passages have in mind is rather the common vicissitudes of life in a sinful and God-hating world in general, and the world's persecution of believers in particular. No-one doubts that the Lord can and does use disease and calamity to chasten His children in the short term, especially if they are being disobedient and unfaithful to him (e.g. Ps. 119:67-71). But Peter specifically states that Christians should not regard this as God's perfect will for them (I Pet. 2:20; 3:17; 4:13-16). And James, for instance, distinguishes affliction or suffering in general from sickness or disease in particular (Jas. 5:13-14). He declares the Lord's willingness to heal those who have sinned if they repent and confess their fault (vv. 15-16). In view of these facts, and of the teaching of the whole Bible regarding God's willingness to heal (which is set out in more detail in the following chapter), it is surely unwarranted to urge sickness upon believers as part of God's perfect will of suffering. It cannot be said to be part of the sufferings of Christ in which we can share, since His only personal experience of sickness appears to have been vicariously on the cross for us (see below p. 38f. on Isa. 53). Even allowing for the possibility of Satanic assault on the believer at this physical

18

level (as in the case of Job, who is instanced as an example of steadfast patience in Jas. 5 : 11 — see further pp. 24-5 and Appendix C, pp. 61ff.), there seems no warrant in Scripture for expecting anything more than permitted short-term afflictions by disease for this purpose, for those who walk uprightly and in prayerful trust with God. Of course, if there is a conflict, due to disobedience or anything else, between wholeness at the spiritual level and wholeness at the physical level, there can be no doubt which must take precedence under the discipline of sonship, for the spiritual is always paramount. But that such a conflict is inevitable and desirable in an obedient and faithful child of God under normal circumstances, is unproven from the word of God. Indeed, in so far as it tends to undermine positive faith in God's promises of healing, we feel bound to reject it. To a more detailed consideration of those promises and of their background, meaning and appropriation we now turn.

2. Biblical teaching on disease and healing

Sickness, Disease, Disability, Deformity etc.

Besides what we have already seen about the law or rule of sin and death and Satan, Job 1 and 2 and Acts 10: 38 (e.g.) show that Satan is generally regarded as responsible for plaguing mankind with disease and destruction, so that it is not surprising that death and Hades are going to end up in the same state as the devil (Rev. 20: 10, 14-15). Nevertheless God is still sovereign, and in His providence can use evil to produce good; and He does so with disease and death as with other things, often using them as a judgement, chastisement, or warning to call people to repentance. Hence death and disease can be spoken of as either a satanic affliction or a divine visitation (or both), especially in the Old Testament, but also in the New (e.g. 1 Cor. 11:29-32).

The Old and New Testaments both show an awareness that the root causes of disease are often spiritual and emotional, rather than physical. In fact, the idea that disease is just a physical phenomenon is quite unknown to the biblical writers. Modern medicine is now very aware of psychosomatic disorders and disease, and therefore is learning to treat man as a unity, a single whole person, and not just a conglomeration of parts and symptoms. The word of God, however, has taught this all along. See Pss. 31: 9-10; 32:3-4; 38:3-11; Prov. 12:4, 18, 25; 14:30; 15:30; 16:24; 17:22; 18:21 etc.; Mark 2:1-12; Jas. 5:14-16. These passages will repay careful study by anyone engaged in a healing ministry. There are too many to print in full, but here are one or two typical verses from them.

"There is no soundness in my flesh because of thy indignation;
    there is no health in my bones because of my sin . . .
My wounds grow foul and fester because of my foolishness,
    I am utterly bowed down and prostrate . . .

> My heart throbs, my strength fails me;
> and the light of my eyes — it has gone from me . . .
> I am ready to fall, and my pain is ever with me;
> I confess my iniquity, I am sorry for my sin . . ."

"My eye is wasted from grief, my soul and my body also . . ."

"There is one whose rash words are like sword thrusts, but the tongue of the wise brings healing . . ."

"A tranquil mind gives life to the flesh, but passion makes the bones rot."

"A cheerful heart is a good medicine, but a downcast spirit dries up the bones."

In the wider sense, of course (possibly barring some "accidental" breakages and damage) all disease is pneumato-somatic. But this does not mean that all sickness etc. is due to sin by the individual or their parents. (See Job and John 9:1ff., where sickness was God's opportunity to glorify His Name.)

Christ appears to have regarded sickness as an evil to be alleviated, overcome, cured and dispelled wherever possible (cf. Luke 13:16 — the woman with the bent back — and Acts 10:38, where satanic connections are mentioned — and the many instances where disabilities are attributed to satanic spirits, e.g. of deafness and dumbness).

Healing

It is our conviction that healing at every level of the person (including the physical) is part of God's provision of salvation during this New Tesament age of grace. Besides the reasons already outlined above (the unity of man, of death, of life and of salvation in Christ), the following areas of study lend more detailed and weighty support to this conclusion:

(a) *The promises and action of God in the Old Testament*
There are not many specific and individual cases of healing recorded in the Old Testament, though there are several examples of the staying of plagues, the averting of judge-

ments (e.g. the brazen serpent in Num. 21:4-9 etc.), and of individuals being healed, such as Naaman, David, Job, Hezekiah and others. But there is a lot of material on healing and health in the way of teaching and promises. In the Old Testament, God's people were promised healing, health and length of days if they walked with Him, but sickness, death and pestilence if they did not. Here are a few examples, among others:

"There the Lord made for them a statute and an ordinance and there he proved them, saying, 'If you will diligently hearken to the voice of the Lord your God, and do that which is right in His eyes, and give heed to His commandments and keep all His statutes, I will put none of the diseases upon you which I put upon the Egyptians; for I am the Lord, your healer' " (Exod. 15:25-26).

"You shall serve the Lord your God, and I will bless your bread and your water; and I will take sickness away from the midst of you. None shall cast her young or be barren in your land; I will fulfil the number of your days" (Exod. 23: 25-26).

"And the Lord will take away from you all sickness; and none of the evil diseases of Egypt, which you knew, will He inflict upon you, but He will lay them upon all who hate you") (Deut. 7:15 *in loc.*).

See also Deut. 28, which also lists the blessings of obedience and the curses of disobedience, among which all kinds of mental and physical sickness figure prominently, and Psalm 91, which dwells on the blessings of trustful living in the Lord's presence, including protection from plague, pestilence and disease.

"Bless the Lord, O my soul, and forget not all His benefits.

Who forgives all your iniquity, who heals all your diseases,

Who redeems your life from the pit,

Who crowns you with steadfast love and mercy,

Who satisfies you with good as long as you live,

So that your youth is renewed like the eagle's" (Ps. 103: 2-5).

See also Ps. 107:17-20; and Prov. 3:1-2, 7-8 and 16; 4:10, 20-23. Here the emphasis is more upon the health-giving commandments of God's wisdom bringing "life to those who find them, and healing to all their flesh".

Other means of healing are not mentioned, but from the instances where we see these promises acted upon with a view to healing, the main means seem to be repentance and prayer, often allied to sacrifice.

The question is sometimes raised as to whether healing is among God's "covenanted" or "uncovenanted" mercies — that is, whether it is something promised to all God's people, or whether it is simply dispensed in His sovereign and uncovenanted grace to whom He chooses among them. The difficulties in accepting the first alternative will be dealt with later on in this book, but here are some reasons for asserting it to be the correct one.

(i) The promises given on this subject are no more and no less conditional or restricted than any other promises belonging to God's covenant, and indeed they are not infrequently stated side by side with such promises (e.g. Ps. 103: 3). We cannot therefore say that they were not open to all of God's people without at the same time denying the openness of the promises of the other blessings of salvation.

(ii) The compound covenant title used in Exod. 15:26, *Yahweh-rāphā* "The Lord (who) heals" — is one of seven such titles which are compounded with God's covenant name *Yahweh* (or Jehovah) in the Old Testament, all of which serve as promises to His people as a whole and without discrimination. The other six are *Yahweh-yirĕh* (the Lord will provide); *Yahweh-nissi* (the Lord is my banner); *Yahweh-rā'āh* (the Lord is my shepherd), *Yahweh-shālōm* (the Lord is peace), *Yahweh-tsidhkēnu* (the Lord is our righteousness), and *Yahweh-shammāh* (the Lord is there) (Gen. 22:14; Exod. 17:15; Ps. 23:1; Judg. 6:23-4: Jer.

23:6 and 33:16; Ezek. 48:35). There seems no good reason for limiting the extent and validity of one without doing the same for all the rest (for which no good reason can be given either). It is surely as much a covenanted promise as the others are.

(iii) This is not seen as ceasing under the New Covenant. The remarkable prophecies of Isaiah and others, particularly chapters 35 and 53, foretell the coming new age as one in which diseases and disabilities would be healed, and our pains and sickness would be borne by the Messianic Servant of Yahweh. In view of the ministry of Jesus Christ, it would be foolish to make this merely a case of prophecy foretelling the future in terms of the past. Nor should the fact that another prophet, Jeremiah, sometimes uses disease and healing as a picture of spiritual sin and salvation, blind us to the reality of God's promises concerning physical and mental disease and healing in the Old Testament; in fact, this prepares us somewhat for the New Testament view of salvation and the kingdom.[8]

We may also note here again the comprehensiveness of the Old Testament concepts of "life" and of "peace" as noted by many writers, including, for example, C. Ryder Smith in *The Bible Doctrine of Grace* (Epworth 1956), chapters 2 and 3. On the one hand the promises of life, and the commands to seek it, present spiritual and physical life without distinction as aspects of one whole concept (see further Appendix A, p. 55ff.), and on the other *shālōm* (peace) covers well-being at every level and in every relationship, and is translated ten times in the Greek Septuagint by a term like "to be in good health" (*hugiainein*) amongst others. It is well known that these two terms ("life" and "peace") summarize, as much as any others, the blessings of God's covenant salvation in the Old and New Testaments. On the other hand, the case of Job prevents us from concluding dogmatically that health and righteousness are always coterminous in an individual's experience, and introduces us to the unseen spiritual forces of Satan

24

seeking man's destruction and death. Let us not forget, however, that Job himself was healed. (See further Appendix C on *Job and the problem of the prosperity of the wicked,* p. 61.)

Before passing on to the New Testament evidence, we simply pose this question:

If the New is a better Covenant, dare we expect God to be less willing to be gracious on any level then He was under the Old, especially in view of the ministry of Jesus Christ?

(b) *The Ministry of Christ*

(i) The Healings

Christ's ministry abounded in healings; about a quarter of the gospels are concerned with this side of His ministry (see Appendix D, p. 67ff.). The healings under His ministry seem to have been very quick, if not always instantaneous. Although He did not heal all in Judaea who were sick, He *never* turned anyone away, or refused to heal those who came to Him for healing, unless it was to have more time to pray for His Father's power (Luke 5: 15-17). Many times we read that He healed them *all* and that He healed *all kinds* of disease (e.g. Matt. 4:23; 9:35; Mark 6:56; Luke 4:40; 6:19; 9:11). The only thing that seems to have prevented Him was unbelief (Matt. 13:57-58; Mark 6:5-6). In the mind of Christ and of those who came to Him, faith included a conviction of His, and therefore of God's, *willingness,* as well as ability, to heal (e.g. Matt. 8:1-13; Mark 9:14-29; — N.B. vv. 22-24). The only time that the two were ever separated (by the leper in Matt. 8:1-4), at the outset of His ministry Jesus made clear His willingness as well as ability to heal. Healings were both an expression of Christ's compassion and evidence of His Person, authority, message and kingdom, and hence of His Father's also. The idea that the compassion and power of God can or should be divorced from each other is completely foreign to the

25

ministry of Jesus to those in need, as well as to His teaching of all but the proud, unloving and hypocritical.

(ii) Christ's teaching

Concerning the kingdom of God, Christ clearly taught that the healing of disease and the deliverance from Satanic powers that was often necessary to that end, was one aspect and evidence of the overthrow of Satan's kingdom by the reign and power of God (Matt. 12:28; Luke 11:20). He saw the "signs" or "works", as He described the miracles, as a stepping-stone to faith (John 10:37-38; 14:10-11) and stressed their value as evidence, not only to convert to faith in Him and His word, but also to render culpable those who refused to believe (Matt. 11:20-24; John 15:24).

The use of the term *sēmeion* ("sign") by John to describe Christ's miracles has been somewhat narrowly interpreted by some people. They rightly point out that many of these miracles in John have a spiritual and parabolic significance, and form a kind of text for a sermon, e.g. John chapters 6, 8-9, and 11; and they then draw the unwarranted conclusion that the signs are, therefore, *only symbolic* of the nature of the kingdom of God. But surely the word "sign" can equally well mean a *token instancing* of the general case by a particular, and is not necessarily the *symbolic representation* of *one* thing by *another*. Christ's words on the kingdom quoted earlier suggest this view, rather than the purely symbolic.[9] The healing of disease and the casting out of demons do not merely *symbolize* the arrival of God's kingdom and salvation, they themselves evidence and *exemplify* it.

Christ also used the word *sōzō* to mean equally "save" or "make whole", implying that healing is as much a part of *sōtēria* (salvation) as forgiveness (Mark 5:28 and 34; 10:52; Luke 7:50 etc.; the same usage, incidentally, occurs by Peter in Acts 4:9-12). The forgiveness and healing of the paralytic in Mark 2:1-12 would obviously be a strong visual demonstration of this fact.

26

(iii) Christ's Commissions

The various commissions of Christ to His disciples, and his statements regarding the church's ministry after His ascension, can be studied in the following passages:

Mission of the Twelve: Matt. 9:35 to 10:8; Mark 6:7-13; and Luke 9:1-6.

Mission of the Seventy: Luke 10:1-20 (and N.B. verses 21-25).

Statements on the night of His arrest: John 14:9-14 (N.B. especially verse 12).

His parting commission: Matt. 28:17-20, (Mark 16:15-20), Luke 24:46-49; John 20:21-23; and Acts 1:1-8.

From the first two sets of passages, His commissions to the twelve and the seventy, the following facts are clear: Jesus gave the disciples or apostles authority over *all* demonic powers, and to heal *every* sort of disease. On that basis He instructed them to heal the sick, cleanse the lepers, raise the dead and cast out demons; as they did this, they were to preach the advent of God's kingdom, of which these works were evidence. The necessity of faith on the part of those healed is not stressed, though the acceptance or rejection of Christ's disciples is.

The disciples at that time had not personally received, or been baptized in, the Holy Spirit (John 7:37-39). Therefore the power by which they were enabled to execute Christ's commissions on those occasions must have been an extension of the anointing of the Holy Spirit which was upon Jesus personally for His ministry on earth from the time of His baptism in the Jordan. However, lest we should conclude that His instructions to them for those missions are no longer relevant after His earthly ministry has ceased, Jesus' promises to His disciples in the third section (John 14:9ff.) are designed specifically to reassure us on that point. After His ascension the same Holy Spirit is coming to be with them for ever — indeed Jesus Himself is coming in the person of the Spirit, unlimited now by earthly conditions. Therefore as they pray in His name they will do the same works as Jesus did, and greater, and so they and the Spirit will bear witness, and the world will be convinced (14:12-18; 15:26-27; 16:8-11). "Truly, truly, I tell you, he that believes in me will also do the works that I do, and greater works than these will he do, because I go to the Father" — to be crowned King of kings, and to receive the Spirit to pour out on the church (14:12). This is not confined to the apostles, and "works" in John clearly means His miraculous works (compare vv. 10-11; 5:36; 10:25, 37, 38; 15:24). If John 14:9 is true, and Christ shows us the Father perfectly in this as in other respects, we cannot surely believe that the Father has changed, or that Christ has, in their attitude to sin or disease or people, any more than in anything else. In that case surely we should expect His mighty "works" to continue through the church down the ages (compare Heb. 13:8). Indeed, putting Luke 10:16 in its context, and taking it together with Christ's remarks in John 10:37-38, we may even ask whether it is possible for a person actually to reject Christ without having seen any evidence of His "works". Certainly it seems to have been far from His recorded intention that this necessity should be laid upon people; and He specifically stated that He did not expect people necessarily to believe in Him apart from the evidence of His "works".

When we come to the fourth group of passages — His parting commissions to the disciples prior to His ascension — this picture is considerably re-inforced. The issue is sometimes debated as if it were simply a question of the genuineness of the longer ending of Mark. Whilst the textual evidence is against it being the original ending of that Gospel, the present writer would regard it as early and a genuine account, being instanced in all but one particular (the drinking of poison) in the subsequent history of the New Testament. If it is accepted, it is clear that Christ's final commission would explicitly include exorcism, healing, glossolalia etc. However, we do not wish to make the case hinge on that point, and there is no reason why it should, since it is clearly implied in the other accounts of the commission. In Matthew, the disciples are told to make disciples and baptize them from all nations, "teaching them to observe all things whatsoever I have commanded you". Plainly in the disciples' minds this "all things" must have included healing and exorcism as in their previous commissions, a ministry they evidently exercised on other occasions after the missions. (See Matt. 17:14ff. and parallels — their question in v. 19 shows their surprise at their failure on this particular occasion). In John 20:21-23, the disciples are sent by Jesus on the same mission in this world, with the same authority, and equipped with the same power, as Jesus Himself was by the Father. The fact that only the forgiveness and retention of sins is specifically mentioned is neither here nor there, after chapter 14. They all knew they were to bear witness and preach and do Jesus' works, *just as* He had been sent to do His Father's. In Luke 24 and Acts 1 essentially the same picture emerges; repentance and forgiveness are stressed, and the empowering of the Spirit. What for? So that Jesus may continue "both to do and teach", as He had begun to up to that point. The continuance of His works is no less expected by Luke - Acts than by the others. The implication of the place of healing in our Lord's commissions seems quite clear. He would continue with His disciples, His church, continuing to do and teach through them, continuing His prophetic and kingly ministry of compassion and power. The evidence of the New Testament favours this expectation, and there seems very little, if anything, to indicate the reverse.

(c) *The early church*

(i) Acts

There are many healings and miracles here, which take place not only through apostles (e.g. Ananias, Philip — Acts 8 and 9). Again, there are instances of *all* being healed (e.g. Acts 3:1 - 4:12; 5:12-16; 8:5-13; 9:32-43; 14:3 and 8-10; 19:11ff.; 20:9-12; 28:8-10). It is note-

worthy that the effect of the demonstration of God's miraculous power, generally in healing, but also on at least two
occasions in judgement, usually causes a widespread turning to the Lord as Saviour. Again we notice that faith is
at least sometimes looked for in the person being healed,
e.g. Acts 14:9. How did it come? Presumably because
Paul preached Christ as the Saviour of the whole person,
including the Healer of the body (compare Rom. 10:17). It
seems from the Acts evidence that some miracles of healing took place in the sovereignty of God, without human
instrumentality; some on the initiative of the Holy Spirit
through the person ministering with a gift of healing or
faith or miracles; and some through the faith of respondents
to God's word.

(ii) The Epistles

The Gospel had been preached not in word only, but in
deeds and in power through the Holy Spirit (Rom. 15:18-
19; 1 Cor. 2:1-5; I Thess. 1:5; Heb. 2:3-4). Miracles evidently continued in the churches (Gal. 3:1-5). The church
members, having been baptized in the Holy Spirit, received
gifts of faith, healings, miracle-workings and discernings
of spirits, among others (1 Cor. 12:8ff.). There is the general
expectation that God in Christ would work in people's
bodies as well as their spirits (2 Cor. 4:10-11; Rom. 8:
11).[3] The elders of the church could be called on to pray
and anoint with oil in the name of the Lord (Jesus) with a
view to healing (Jas. 5:14-16 — compare Mark 6:13). The
operative factor which "will save/make whole" here is the
prayer of faith rather than the oil, which is surely symbolic
rather than directly medicinal, since there is no suggestion
that this procedure is confined to the sort of surface wounds
for which the oil might be used medicinally. There is no
indication in this passage that the healing promised will
always be instantaneous. It might well be more gradual.

These verses in James 5 have also considerable import-
ance as the place in the New Testament where *any* believer
30

without distinction is invited to seek the Lord for healing (just as for salvation), and promised it in answer to the prayer of faith by the church, with any necessary confessions and amendment of life on the person's part. This surely re-iterates the Old Testament promises of healing to all believers, and demonstrates that healing is a "covenanted" mercy to the Lord's people under the New Covenant, just as much as under the Old.

This observation prompts us to notice a significant shift in emphasis between the Old and New Testament teaching on healing, which is paralleled by its teaching on the whole of salvation. In the Old Testament, it was almost entirely a question of the promises being there, and people fulfilling the conditions of health, and appropriating them. In the New, that emphasis is still there, especially in the ministry of Christ, in Acts and in James and 1 Corinthians 11. But there is another emphasis, foreshadowed in the Old Testament concept of Israel (and then the remnant, and finally the Messiah) as the servant of Yahweh to the nations. It is the emphasis on the Lord working with and through His people, equipping His disciples/apostles, continuing His ministry through His church — to use St. Paul's phrase, the body of Christ, commissioned by Him, and energized and gifted by His Spirit, to spread His Gospel of salvation-wholeness, the good news of the kingdom, God reigning in men's whole being. Hence to the first basic dimension of the individual's repentance and faith in the healing promises of God and fulfilment of the conditions, there has to be added the other basic dimension of the power of the Lord (the Holy Spirit) being present to heal in and through the body of Christ, as it was in the ministry of Jesus Himself on earth (Luke 5:17; Acts 4:29-31; 5:12ff.). If we neglect this aspect of the matter, our thinking about the healing ministry of Christ today will be seriously defective, and too much of the responsibility for healing will be placed on the shoulders of the individuals seeking healing.

3. Some questions answered

Factors Affecting the Individual's Enjoyment of the Promises of God regarding Salvation-Wholeness

The individual's enjoyment of the blessings of salvation and of the covenant at any one time and in any particular age are affected by several factors. These include, but go beyond, the individual's own walk with God. To grasp this clearly, it is necessary for a moment to consider the different aspects or dimensions of sin and of salvation in this life, and their effects.

First, the *individual* aspect: Salvation has to do with the individual believer or child of God, and he or she is affected in two ways: in his or her relation to God and fellowship with Him, and also in relation to himself or herself. Secondly, the *social or corporate* aspect of salvation: Salvation has to do with men in relation to one another, in community; in the family, home and tribe; in the church; and in the nation and world. The Bible is quite clear that God deals with men both as individuals and as members of a family, society and race. And the effects and repercussions of sin and salvation in curse and blessing affect men in their relationships in time and in space, through the build-up of the generations, and through the community (whether of sin or grace) in which they are set. Thus, for instance, Elijah lacked many of the temporal blessings of prosperity promised to God's obedient people, because of their disobedience in his lifetime, even though at times He was able to rise above the prevailing climate of apostasizing unbelief in Israel, and perform mighty works through prayer and God's gifts and enabling, in pursuance of His word. Thirdly, the *environmental* aspect of salvation: sin and grace affect not only man's relationship to God, to his neighbour and to himself but also to the whole created order of animate and inanimate things (Gen. 3:17ff; Rom. 8:18ff.). Hence we find that God promises to bless or curse the land, crops, flock etc. where men live, according to their individual and com-

32

munal relationship to Him and to one another (Lev. 26; Deut. 28; Hos. 2 etc.).

These factors affect our enjoyment of the fulfilment of God's promises regarding healing, just as much as many other aspects of salvation in this life. Thus a believer set in an unbelieving church, in whatever direction the doubt is operating, will probably experience difficulty in that field, since the health of the body of Christ must affect every member's joy or suffering. Again, a church set in a land where Satan is well served, will have a far more difficult time than a church in a land where, by and large, God is honoured (cf. Rev. chs. 2 and 3). Subject to that understanding and proviso, we can list some of the main factors affecting our enjoyment of healing, along with other blessing of the covenant and of salvation in this life. The main ones seem to be these:

(i) *Faith* — individual and corporate, remember — (see the Gospels *passim*). Under this general heading we include understanding and knowledge of God's word; prayer, sometimes with fasting; using the provisions made by God for our healing in His word; and expectancy, in claiming the present power of the Spirit to apply and fulfil the promises of God, and to equip and gift the church to fulfil the ministry of Christ (see p. 31 above). Perhaps we should add a rider that experience in ministry helps in this area as much as anywhere, and a caution that faith should concentrate on Jesus Christ the Saviour-physician, rather than on any particular gift.

(ii) *Repentance and obedience* (cf. Jas. 5:15-16) — again both individual and corporate. We can include under this heading confession and forsaking of sin, and the need to put right all wrong relationships and attitudes, whether arising out of present situations or carried over from the past life, even from childhood and infancy.[10] The author's own experience has shown time and again the need of the healing of past griefs and sorrows by Christ, if such things are to be put right and physical healing is to be achieved. We need to beware of a magical attitude to the healing promises of God, and treat people as *people,* not just as bodies, nor simply as spirits. Equally, notice Jesus' question to a man who had been ill 38 years (John 5), "Do you *want* to be healed (or 'made whole')?". There must be a willingness to face the consequences and adjustments of being healed (such as leaving behind over-dependence, diminished responsibility, and self-pity), and a resolve to do God's will with all one's powers.

(iii) *The sovereign hand of God our Father, and under that, the operations of the devil and his powers being thoroughly dealt with.* One has noticed that an involvement in occultism and idolatry often holds people back from healing until specifically confessed, repented of and renounced.[11] The Bible shows that the devil is allowed a certain amount of rope by God, and his forces attack people from within and without. If a demon or spirit needs casting out, we must be prepared to do it.[12] Equally we have to pray away the assaults of Satan on the minds and bodies of believers. But God is in final control, and one notices that He dictates the means of healing in any particular case. Sometimes, for reasons not always apparent to us, although doubtless in general keeping with the outline and factors observed already in this study (which would adequately account for most, if not all, so-called "failures" in healing), He allows Christian people to die before a full life-span has been lived out, from sickness as well as by war, famine or persecution. Such cases are no cause for complacency about the healing ministry, but in many of them we can only bow in the presence of the One Who knows all things and is Lord of life and death, and rejoice in their certain hope of a better resurrection.[13]

Summary of New Testament Means of Healing

The following modes of healing are exemplified:

(a) The sovereignty of God without other noticeable human means (though this may often have been in answer to someone's prayers in the background).

(b) The laying on of hands (e.g. Mark 6:5; Acts 28: 8).

(c) A command or announcement in Christ's name (either a rebuke, or "arise" or "be whole", e.g. Luke 4:39; Acts 9:34).

(d) The prayer of faith. Notice this *"will"* save or make whole (Jas. 5:15), not *"may"*, therefore it must be a prayer of confidence in God's will to heal (compare Mark 11:22-24; 1 John 5:14-15). Unless faith is to be made into a private hunch at the prompting of the Spirit and disjoined from the word of God, surely the prayer of faith must be based upon the promises of God (Rom. 10:17).

(e) Anointing with oil in the name of the Lord (Jesus) symbolizing presumably the healing power of the Holy Spirit (Mark 6:13; Jas. 5:14).

(f) The Word of God calling forth faith (e.g. Acts 14:3, 8-9).

(g) Other outward signs (spittle, clay etc. e.g. Mark 7:31-37; John 9:6-7). These occur mainly in the ministry of Jesus, though in Acts 19:11-12 "extraordinary miracles" are performed through cloths and aprons sent from Paul to the sick.

(h) People making some sort of physical contact with Jesus or His disciples in faith — e.g. touching the hem of Christ's garment, or Peter's shadow etc. (Matt. 9:20; 14:35-36; Acts 5:15-16).

Possible Objections or Causes for Concern

In the face of the mass of New Testament evidence in favour of healing, contrary objections are adduced by some from the following passages:

Epaphroditus in Phil. 2:25-30, who was "ill and near to

death". This seems irrelevant, since "God had mercy on him" and healed him after his severe illness, and therefore proves nothing.

Timothy's stomach in I Tim. 5:23:

"No longer drink only water, but use a little wine for the sake of your stomach and your frequent ailments". This merely shows that we are expected to be sensible, and use any means which are to hand; not to use prayer as a substitute for common sense (or disciplined living). (Water in eastern and Mediterranean countries is still frequently not pure enough to drink safely.) The Bible does not forbid recourse to doctors. There is no evidence that Luke renounced his profession as a physcian because he became a Christian, and it is surely basic to a biblical view of God and the world that the God of miracles, grace and salvation is also the God of creation, means and natural science.

The case of Asa in the Old Testament (2 Chron. 16:12), who is condemned because "even in his disease he did not seek the Lord, but sought help from the physicians" is not against this, because Asa's condemnation is basically for *not seeking* the Lord. He would only be condemned for seeking physicians, either because he sought healing from them while running away from God and His will, and without prayer, or because the physicians themselves may have been occult practitioners in league with the idolatrous forces of Satan. Jeremiah's remarks about the balm and physician of Gilead are a precise parallel to this case (Jer. 8:22 *in loc.,* and other similar passages in chapters 8, 14, 30 and 46). These references are also a strong reminder, if we need it, that God is not interested merely in physical wholeness but in the salvation-healing of the whole person, in which the spiritual relationship to God and His word is obviously paramount (compare Mark 2:1-12 and Jas. 5:14-16).

Paul's thorn in the flesh (2 Cor. 12:1-9):

The assumption that Paul's thorn in the flesh here was a physical disease seems at the very least unproven, probably unnecessary, and perhaps even unwarranted. The tendency of some commentators to connect this passage with "his infirmity of the flesh" and trouble with his eyes at Galatia (Gal. 4:12-16) presumably rests upon the use of the word *asthēneia* (infirmity or weakness). However, a brief glance at the use of this word and its cognates in the Greek Testament will show that it is by no means confined to physical disease. It can even be used of God in 1 Cor. 1:25. The term "thorn in the flesh" appears to be taken from Num. 33:55 and Josh. 23:13, where the reference is a personal one, to the peoples of the land, and has nothing to do with disease. The phrase "an angel (or messenger) of Satan" would surely rather speak of demonic onslaughts, such as stirring up of persecution and other troubles, than of disease. Furthermore, there is no evidence (apart from considerably later references by church historians) that Paul's eye trouble at Galatia was due to anything other than his stoning in Acts 14:19, or that he had it permanently thereafter. Some have sought support for that view from Gal. 6:11, "See with what large letters I have written to you with my own hand," arguing that the reason for his large handwriting was his near blindness. It is, of course, possible that the effects of his stoning were still with him in this way when he wrote the letter fairly soon after being with them (1:6), and that this was one of the "marks of the Lord Jesus" he bore in his body at that time (6:17). However, we know from others of his letters that it was his normal practice to use an amanuensis to write his letters out for him, and then to conclude with a final "greetings" paragraph in his own handwriting (see 1 Cor. 16:21; Col. 4:18; 2 Thess. 3:17). Therefore it is likely that he is merely pointing out the contrast between the fine and neat hand of his amanuensis and his own somewhat larger, less "professional" script. Any supposition beyond this must remain pure speculation, and quite insufficient as grounds for discrediting the biblical promises of healing. It certainly seems extremely unlikely that anybody would have received faith to be healed

through the preaching of someone whose whole bodily appearance ("eyes suppurating" etc.[14]) would have testified in
the opposite direction.

Trophimus (2 Tim. 4:20):

"Trophimus I left ill at Miletus."

The reason for Trophimus' illness and whether he was sub-
sequently healed is simply not known. In the face of such
ignorance, it would seem somewhat unwise to build a whole
doctrine of non-healing on half a verse in the New Testament, in view of all the other evidence.

Is There Healing in the Atonement?

(i) The verses which are invoked in support of this are
particularly Matt. 8:17 (*in loc.*), based on Isa. 53:3ff. where
the words *chōli* and *mākōb* are translated "griefs" and "sorrows" in our English version. F. F. Bosworth, in "Christ
the Healer",[15] correctly points out that Matthew's interpre-
tation of the words to mean pains and disease are simply
respect for the actual meaning of the original words. A few
minutes with a good concordance will show any candid
reader that *chōli* is properly translated "disease" or "sickness" in the vast majority of cases in the Old Testament,
while *mākōb* can mean equally either "sorrow" or "pain".
The question of whether Christ was bearing our sorrows and
sicknesses on the cross, along with all the other effects and
judgements of sin, cannot be lightly dismissed, since Isaiah
53 is universally recognised as being centred upon Calvary;
the same words *nāsā* ("bear") and *sābal* ("carry") are both
used of iniquities, and of sorrows and disease; and the
representative and substitutionary trend of the passage
seems clear. This latter emphasis appears to be related explicitly to healing and wholeness in verses 5 and 10, where
we read ". . . Upon him was the chastisement that made us
whole, and with his stripes we are healed", and ". . . it was
the will of the Lord to bruise him; He has made him
sick . . ." (see the margin note on the meaning of the Hebrew
phrase). Even if "bear" and "carry" in Matt. 8:17 are taken

38

to mean "lift away" (by healing)[16], yet in Isaiah 53, the whole concept is so closely bound up together with the atonement (including its representative and substitutionary aspects), that the two ideas cannot be severed without doing violence to the prophet's thought.

(ii) Certain Old Testament sacrifices, types, and incidents bring into particular prominence the connection between atonement and healing. Three examples will suffice: (a) the sacrifices for the cleansing of leprosy in Lev. 14 and 15 (notice especially 14:1-9, and the picture of the two birds[17], so close to the goats of the Day of Atonement in chapter 16). Unless we are going to assert that leprosy is *always* the result of personal sin, or to treat it as *nothing more* than a type of sin, the implications are inescapable. (b) The bronze serpent in Num. 21:4-9. This is taken up by Christ in John 3:14ff. as a type of His atonement at the cross. Yet the people were commanded to look upon this type — a dead bronze replica of the snake whose deadly bite had touched them — not merely for forgiveness, but also for healing of their plague. (Compare e.g. Num. 25:7-13, and 2 Sam. 24:25 *in loc.*). (c) Elihu's words in Job 33:23-25 seem to be based, like some of David's words in the Psalms (e.g. Ps. 49), on the concept of an atoning 'ransom' (*kōpher*) bringing healing, wholeness and life again.

(iii) Besides these considerations, it is surely clear that all the blessings which flow to us in Christ must flow through His atoning meditation in any case. The only grounds for debate are therefore: (a) whether the healing or salvation-wholeness promised and secured for us by our Lord Jesus at Calvary is simply to be understood as physical healing (or any other particular sort), or whether we understand this healing and wholeness in its full biblical scope, as including these particular aspects but also greatly transcending them. We have shown that the latter is the only possible view if we are to be faithful to Scripture. (b) Whether, secondly, healing is "covenanted" or "uncovenanted" mercy or blessing from God. This question has been partially treated on pages 23-24, but we can now add that provided we take the full biblical view of salvation and wholeness outlined earlier (and therefore draw the right conclusion under (a) above), the fact that the atonement secures healing for us makes it undoubtedly a covenanted blessing of the Lord.

In order to round off the question of healing as a "covenanted", as opposed to "uncovenanted", mercy from God, we may add to the two grounds already adduced (the Covenant names *Yahweh-Rāphā* and *Yahweh-Shālōm* — see p. 23f. — and the atonement) two further considerations: (a) We take the view that the ministry of Jesus Christ (and of His Apostles) must determine our knowledge of the blessings vouchsafed to believers under the New Covenant. This is argued in more detail later (pages 50ff.). Suffice it to say here that Jesus and His ministry show us the Father (John 14:9), that He is the same yesterday today and forever (Heb. 13:8), and that the New Testament itself gives every ground for expecting the continuance of His ministry through the church, and no definite hint of the reverse. (b) The promises of God, including His promises of healing to us in this life, are "generally" given (i.e. open promises to all His people — all who will trust and follow Him) and therefore are to be "generally" received. Hence they are open to any Christian to lay hold of (see, for instance, Jas. 5:14: "Is *anyone* among you sick? Let him send . . . and the Lord will raise him up . . ."). If we deny this on the healing promises, we should logically make His other promises of "whosoever will . . ." discriminatory as well. If this conclusion would be wrong, then the premise of denial is clearly false.

Congenital and Accidental Deficiencies and Disabilities

Some Christians, who would accept the possibility of the healing of diseases by Christ, would nevertheless stop short of asserting God's willingness to heal either congenital deficiencies and deformities, including missing organs or limbs as well as faculties, or such disabilities or loss of limbs or organs due to "accidental" casualties or surgery. We should therefore face the question of the relation between "disease" and these other phenomena as far as healing is concerned. There is very little on this subject in the Scriptures, and only a few cases there appear to bear directly upon it. The cases of the man born blind in John 9, and the cripples from birth in Acts 3 and 14 instance the healing of congenital conditions; the raising and healing of Eutychus after a fatal fall in Acts 20:9ff. instances restoration after an accident; and the case of the healing or restoration of Malchus' right ear which had been cut off by a sword in Luke 22:51 probably instances the restoration of an amputated organ. (No details are given of precisely how Christ healed him, except that He touched him. Are we to presume that the ear was miraculously grafted back on, or that a new one grew, or merely that the wound left by the blow was healed and the bleeding staunched?) It is also extremely probable that not a few among the many, many people healed by our Lord during His ministry would have been paralysed and suffering in other ways as a result of accidents. Indeed, one may well wonder whether such distinctions between disease, deformity, deficiency or disability could have been present at all in the mind of either our Lord or the Evangelists. They are largely the product of modern medical science. Many of the conditions Jesus healed would have been the *result* of disease or of accidents rather than a disease in themselves (e.g. paralysis, withered hand, impotent man, bent back etc.). It is unthinkable that He would only have healed people of diseases as such, or that He should have conducted an enquiry into whether the cause of the condition was disease, congenital deficiency or accident, before deciding whether to heal. All we can say is that the replacement of a lost or non-existent organ might be more properly classed as a miracle than a healing, but would nevertheless still be an aspect of making people whole.

In modern times, one knows of cases of the replacement of surgically-removed eardrums instantly after prayer, the lengthening of limbs (in one case nearly six inches instantaneously), and even the growing of a new hand, over a period of several weeks after specific prayer for healing, on the arm of a young girl born without one.[18] The writer does not personally happen to know of the replacement of a whole limb, but that does not mean it could not happen. If God the Creator is able to raise up children for Abraham from stones (Luke 3:8), then certainly nothing along this line is too hard for Him. If we say that whereas the healing of disease is a covenanted blessing, the restoration of limbs, organs and deformities is not (i.e. we must wait till the resurrection for this) — although God is sometimes pleased to do it — we are in a treble difficulty. First, it is doubtful if we are on solid biblical ground (see above); secondly, it is impossible to know where to draw any clear line between the two; and thirdly, the fact is that not a few people who have trusted the Lord for a miracle have been healed or restored in these sorts of ways. (Some might also argue that this is covered in the atonement, in view of Isa. 52:14; and 53:2 and 5.) Which seems to bring us back, both as individuals and even more as a church, to the principle of "according to your faith be it done unto you" (cf. Mark 9:22-23; 11:22ff.). In other words, the possibilities are only limited by what we can believe the Lord for. Surely we need to pray with the first disciples for an increase of faith and of the working of miracles. It is the author's conviction that one of the greatest needs in the church today in respect of the ministry of healing and miracles is for the level and climate of faith and expectancy to be raised.

4. Miracles of healing then and now

The Idea of "Miracle" in the Bible and Today

1. *Miracles in the Bible*
   (a) *The concept of miracles*
If we are to attempt to define the biblical concept of a miracle, we should probably be driven back to a very basic, comprehensive and non-controversial summary definition such as this: "A miracle is a particular kind of physical event, having spiritual significance and value."[19]

Three principal terms are used in the Greek of the New Testament to describe these events:

(i) *Dunamis* — an act of power;

(ii) *Teras* — an eye-catching wonder;

(iii) *Sēmeion* — a sign.

Hence we could summarize the concept of miracle, from the terms used, as "an act of power designed to attract attention as a sign".

(b) *Their types and purpose*
The types of miracle in the Old and New Testaments vary considerably. They may be miracles of judgement (Sodom, Ananias and Sapphira, Elymas etc.), or of mercy (e.g. healings, raising the dead, feeding the 5,000). They may occur in the human, animate or inanimate created order (e.g. the healings, the coin in the fish, walking on the water).

Their purpose varies in its detail, but in general includes the following aspects:

(i) To confront people with the presence and power of God, and in Christ's ministry with the kingdom of God.

(ii) To show the character of God (in compassionate healings, or judgement on sin), and to bless people in accordance with that character.

43

(iii) To carry forward God's purpose in the world.

(iv) To confirm God's word, or authenticate His message or messengers (both fulfilling prophecy and demonstrating the word preached).

(v) To act as parables or visual aids (e.g. John 8 and 9, or John 6, or John 11 — light, bread, life ("signs"?).

(vi) To point to the Messiahship (and divine sonship) of Jesus Christ.

2. *Scientific aspects*

It is impossible to produce one comprehensive "scientific" definition to cover all biblical miracles. We could not simply define them in terms of reversing or contradicting natural or normal physical processes (the so-called "laws of nature", which are really only the Creator's usual way of working in His creation), because they do not necessarily do so. In the case of the Israelites crossing of the Red Sea, for instance, the physical means — a strong east wind which blew all night — is specifically mentioned (Exod. 14:21); the vital thing there is the timing all along.

Most miracles are in any case impossible to "prove" scientifically, since (a) there are too many gaps in our scientific knowledge; (b) they defy classification by their very nature; and (c) they are very rarely "observable" by scientists in any other way than they are observable by "the man in the street".

There is nothing contrary to "science", properly understood, in the concept of the miraculous, unless the scientist has unwarrantably assumed a closed mechanistic universe, of which he has a sufficiently accurate and comprehensive blueprint to enable him to predict completely what is possible under every conceivable circumstance.[20]

3. *Miracles of healing*

The healing miracles are a particular branch of the miraculous especially emphasized and highlighted in Scripture by the ministry of our Lord Jesus Christ.

"When is a healing miraculous?"

The answer to this question may be a matter of degree, according to what is in the mind of the person who asks it. Possible factors which may contribute to the assessment of a particular case of healing as being a miracle might include the following:

(a) No known cure was available or had had any effect (cf. the woman with the issue of blood, and the impotent man of John 5, in the New Testament).

(b) Some people (usually with a medical background) would only be prepared to acknowledge that a healing miracle had occurred when a definite organic (as opposed to functional or psychological) disease or disability had been healed without means.

(c) A healing is so accelerated as to be either instantaneous or almost so (e.g. cancer healed in sleep overnight etc.).

(d) A healing takes place in unlikely circumstances in confirmation of a prophetic word from God, or following a definite claiming of his promises in prayer. The problem here is that while the Christian will see all healing as an answer to prayer, that does not make it wise for him or her to claim all cases of healing which have been prayed for as being miraculous.

It is probably impossible to arrive at a watertight definition in physical and circumstantial terms, although the Roman Catholic Church has wisely tried very hard to satisfy medical and other scepticism and unbelief at this point. We can only finally say that some healings are obviously miraculous; others — even where medical means are not used — are borderline; and others (with or without means) are an answer to prayer, but the miraculous cannot be proved.

Despite the doubts of many doctors, including Christian doctors, one wonders whether there is any real justification in fact for asserting that a healing is less "miraculous" because the basic cause of the disease, disorder or disability was not so much physical as psychological, emotional or spiritual. Is this really a question of evidential value, or simply an instance of confused thinking? The present very limited state of our scientific knowledge of disease, its causes and cure, renders dogmatism over this type of question extremely unwise. The straightforward approach of the Bible, combining faith in the activity of the unlimited God (as Creator and Redeemer) with faith in many ordinary people's common-sense ability to draw the obvious conclusions when confronted with the clear evidence and demonstration of His power, is still surely the safest and best.

4. *Caution — beware of the counterfeit*

Miracles, including miraculous "healings" are sometimes effected by people and forces working for Satan, error and evil, according to Scripture (e.g. Deut. 13:1ff; Matt. 24:24; 2 Thess. 2:9-10). Such "healings" are generally an alleviation or removal of physical or mental symptomatic conditions, and not really a contribution to that wholeness that the Lord wants to give His people. Since Satan is largely responsible for disease according to the Bible, it need not surprise anyone that he can remove it on occasion, when it suits him, and subject to the divine permission.

Whether there is in man an intermediate area of psychic energy in the field of healing due directly neither to the Holy Spirit of Christ, nor to the powers of evil, will doubtless continue to be debated. (The author is personally inclined to doubt it, although we should need to define our terms closely, so as to exclude an unbiblical mechanistic or independent view of man and of the human spirit in the first place.) But the point to be noted well here is simply that the working of miracles, like every other alleged gift of the Spirit, needs testing as to its source and tendency, and all occult streaks in allegedly Christian healing ministries must be steadfastly purged and prayed out, as they are surrendered to the Lord Jesus.[21] The witness of the Word and Spirit of God must agree here as elsewhere.

46

The Raising of the Dead

Another related matter, which must not be passed by in silence, is the raising of the dead, its relation to healing and its place in the commission and ministry of the church. Besides the resurrection of Jesus Christ and the promise of bodily resurrection to a better and fuller life for believers at the last day, and besides the spiritual resurrection which takes place when the Christian is first "born again" and "passes from death to life" (John 5:24-27), there is a good deal in the Bible about the raising of the dead in (or back into) *this* life. We cannot attempt a thorough and exhaustive treatment of this subject here in any sense, but will merely make one or two points in so far as it relates to our general theme.

(i) *The biblical instances.* These are listed at the end of Appendix D on page 69, and include (besides translations), three instances in the Old Testament in the time of Elijah and Elisha, three instances in the earthly ministry of our Lord Jesus Christ, and two instances in the ministry of the apostles. John the Baptist was also specifically told by Christ, that the dead were being raised up (Matt. 11:4-6). None had been dead more than four days, and most had died young, or well before their normal life-span was fulfilled.

(ii) *Our Lord's Commission to His followers* (Matt. 10:8) — on which see above, pages 27ff. — specifically included the command ". . . Raise (the) dead . . ." (cf. also John 14:12). This is a separate command from "Heal the sick" (though related to it), because although it includes the healing of whatever disease the person died of, it is a miracle beyond that, putting life back into the dead. It is therefore a "working of miracles", not just healing.

(iii) *Command, promise and responsibility.* In the case of the raising of the dead, there are no specific promises for believers to lay hold of comparable to those regarding healing. But the risen and glorified Lord Jesus not only holds the keys of death and Hades Himself (Rev. 1:18), but has also committed to His church the keys of the kingdom of heaven with the promise that the gates of Hades shall not prevail against not merely Himself, but also His church (Matt. 16: 18-19). There is nothing in the context to limit this to the final resurrection at the last day, especially if it is based on Wisdom 16:13-14. Plainly, on the part of the person concerned, no faith in such a promise could be exercised anyway, since they are dead! If the family and the church are doing the believing and praying, they are presumably going to base this on the promises concerning the fulfilment of our days or life-span. The initiative, it seems, could come either from the relatives of the dead person, sending for the ministers or prophets concerned (as e.g. in 2 Kings 4:20ff.; Acts 8:36ff.), or from the miracle-worker (prophet, apostle, minister) concerned (as in Luke 7:11ff.; Acts 20:9ff.).

(iv) *Modern instances of such resurrections.* Although the writer has never yet personally witnessed the raising of the dead, yet he knows of at least thirty recorded instances of its occurrence through prayer (sometimes with laying on of hands, or a commanding of death in Jesus' name). The reader is referred for examples to F. L. Wyman's *The Dead are raised up,* K. Koch's *The revival in Indonesia,* and the biography and writings of Smith Wigglesworth.[22]

(v) *The place and need of this miracle.* The primary purpose of this miracle would seem to be two-fold: first and foremost, visibly and unmistakably to demonstrate here and now the victory of the risen Lord Jesus Christ over death and Hades — the power of such a testimony would be hard to exaggerate; secondly, to bring to godly people, prematurely cut off by death, the possibility of fulfilling their days and responsibilities in this life. We need to remember the sovereignty of Jesus Christ here, and to watch and listen for His promptings (John 5:21). Yet the church has a need to take this part of her commission to heart, rather than allowing death invariably to go unchallenged.

Healing and other Miracles in Evangelism

Although the biblical promises of healing are made primarily to God's people as they trust in Jesus Christ, yet the Acts of the Apostles and some of the Epistles make it clear that the healings and other miracles were not confined to Israel, and were in fact one of the main means of advertising the Gospel as it spread on towards "the uttermost parts of the earth". In many cases they were instrumental in causing a very widespread turning to the Lord, as His word was confirmed with signs following (see e.g. Acts 5:12-16; 8:5ff.; 9:33-35, 36-42; 14:3ff., 10ff; 19:11-20; 28:7ff.). In the light of the commissions of Christ and the book of Acts, healing and miracles plainly have a place in evangelism. This can be summarized as being meant to come about in three or four ways: (i) Those who believe in Christ as Saviour and Lord are prayed for and get healed; (ii) Jesus is presented as the Saviour of the whole person, including His ministry as the great Physician; (iii) Many people touch Him in faith at the point of their physical or mental need first, and so are healed (they need of course to go on to accept Him as Saviour and Lord so that He can make them whole "from their spirit outwards"); (iv) God the Holy Spirit will prompt His ministers to lay hands on the sick or raise the dead, for a testimony to those hearing the good news, or will simply do it sovereignly Himself as the word is preached.

Some of the most remarkable results have attended the bold full preaching of the Gospel in this way in the power of the Spirit in this century, especially, but by no means only, in pioneer mission situations.[23] It is our conviction that the working man throughout the world will be convinced by deeds rather than words. There is a need once again to preach the Gospel "not in word only" but "in the power of signs and wonders, by the power of the Holy Spirit", or "in demonstration of the Spirit and of power" (1 Thess. 1:5; Rom. 15:18-19; 1 Cor. 2:4-5). On page 28 above, we posed the question whether people can really be said to have heard or seen Christ properly, so as meaningfully to reject Him when they reject His messengers and word, if they have seen no evidence of His works. Certainly if we set Matthew 10:14 and Luke 10:16 in their context, we see clearly that Christ never intended those who heard His Gospel of the Kingdom to be placed in such a position.

The Question of Church History

B. B. Warfield and others have argued that the day of miracles and of divine healing, apart from doctors, is past and ought to be so.[24] Warfield's main argument is from church history rather than from the New Testament, and it can be summarized as follows: Miracles and miraculous gifts ceased in the church after the first three centuries of the church's history, and possibly even earlier, and have never re-appeared on any wide scale. This is to be explained by the fact that they were only meant to be connected with the original apostles and their mission, and therefore these gifts and miracles were withdrawn after the apostolic (and possibly sub-apostolic) era, and any supposed subsequent appearance of them is to be rejected or explained away as spurious. Others have modified Warfield's position, and accept the connection of the miraculous gifts with the founding of the church, but allow for their reappearance here and there at odd times in the subsequent history of the church, as for instance in some periods of spiritual revival and awakening. (Some would add an expectation of a wider outpouring towards the end of the age.) All these views place the occurrence or non-occurrence of these miraculous phenomena entirely within the inscrutable sovereignty of God, who simply either bestows or withholds them at His supreme good pleasure.

Leaving aside the tendency of Warfield to squeeze the historical evidence somewhat in order to make it fit his own particular dogmatic mould,[25] this whole debate focusses several theological questions or problems posed by the phenomena of church history. Many people who freely acknowledge the sovereignty of almighty God in history, have

50

nevertheless realized that to place the whole question solely within the sphere of divine sovereignty, denying the place of human faith and responsibility, is theologically unbalanced. They further observe that the New Covenant is not divided up by Scripture into dispensations (charismatic or otherwise), and that gifts have to be desired and received as well as given (1 Cor. 14:1). It is therefore arguable that such miraculous gifts were always in principle available to the church throughout the New Covenant era, but that what the church did not seek, expect or claim, was not very widely experienced. Indeed, the Warfield-type views entirely fail to explain why the New Testament tells us to *desire* such gifts (1 Cor. 12:31; 14:1). Had Warfield lived today, he would almost certainly have had to modify his position, in the light of undeniable phenomena which have appeared in the Pentecostal and charismatic movements of this century. For a major theological problem confronting those who adopt such an attitude is, what to make of the charismatic phenomena of the present century. They are forced to explain these away as either satanic counterfeits or else in purely psychological terms — a position which so increasingly lacks credibility as to convince none but those determined to hold on to it at all costs.

The major theological problem or challenge presented to those who believe that miraculous healing (and/or other charismatic phenomena) is for today, may be stated thus: Why, when God is gracious beyond all that we ask or think (or believe for) in so many other respects, has He not poured forth healing and other miracles in more widespread profusion down the history of the church, if all these things were intended by Him for the church in every age? To this, three facts can be adduced in reply.

(i) Although some of the things discussed by Warfield in church history after the fourth century are plainly either counterfeit or purely psychological, by no means all the recorded phenomena of church history can be so easily dismissed as he supposes.[26] (Quite apart from this, of course, no-one has any accurate means of knowing how much of the works of God in the history of the church is actually recorded for posterity in "church history's" written records — see John 21:25).

(ii) Charismatic gifts and miraculous healings have been seen and experienced in some periods of revival. Yet often the prevailing theology and preaching explained this purely in terms of the sovereignty of God, or worse still, took no account at all of His promises along these lines. As a result, no-one felt any responsibility for the continuance or prolonged exercise (let alone increase) of the charismata and healings, when the visitation of God's Spirit waned. Hence it is not surprising if they fairly quickly ceased or died out, and were then said to have been "withdrawn".

(iii) This experience in relation to healing and the charismata can be paralleled to some extent by other aspects of church history — for example, the failure of the church for long periods in many lands to experience Christian assurance, because the teaching given precluded any general possibility of it. Hence we do not believe that church history provides any unanswerable problems for the account of the biblical teaching on healing and miracles which is presented in this book.

Miracles and Healing in the Bible and Today

Although Warfield's main argument is from church history, he and others also argue their case from the Bible, and their principal scriptural arguments for it appear to be three or four-fold. First, they point out that miracles in the Bible occur in spates at times of crisis or of new revelation (i.e. Moses, Elijah and Elisha, and Jesus Christ). This may be largely true of the Old Testament, but the new Messianic age was predicted as being an age of miracles when the Holy Spirit is poured out on all flesh (e.g. Isa. 35; Joel 2). The fact that it was ushered in supernaturally in no sense proves that it was not meant to be continued in the same way.

52

Secondly, it is argued that Christ's miracles were simply there to attest His own personal authority, and that therefore the same sort of things may not be expected in any other ministry. To the present writer's mind, this both narrows the purpose of the healing miracles and also flies in the face both of the words of Jesus and of the evidence of the New Testament. The healings were to confront people with the presence and power of God and to demonstrate the presence of His kingdom. No-one can convincingly argue that this need is not present today. The miracles also show the character of God (in compassionate healings, or in judgement on sin). Further, they confirm Christ's word and authenticate His ministry.

Thirdly, St. Paul's statement in 2 Cor. 12:12 about "the signs of an apostle" are taken to mean that the miracles, works and signs are confined to Christ and His personally appointed apostles, as the founders of the church universal. This does not follow from the verse, both because the term "apostle" has a wider and a narrower sense in the Bible, and also because the New Testament speaks of gifts of healing and miracles given generally to the church, in confirmation of Christ's promise to those who believe on Him. The fact that these ministries were combined in the person of an apostle in no sense means that they may not be found anywhere else.

Another argument sometimes used is that the gifts of healings, etc. were meant to disappear, along with other charismatic gifts such as tongues, prophecy and the word of knowledge, as is stated in 1 Cor. 13:8-13. However, this argument is ill-founded, since there is nothing said in that passage about *when* these gifts will have passed away, except that they will have done so when "the perfect has come", when "we see face to face", and when "we know even as we are known". Such a state of affairs can hardly be thought to obtain in the church on earth at the present time.

God in Christ is still the same, the living God, who speaks

and acts. Each generation and each nation needs to see and hear His Gospel afresh. Human need is still much the same, and medical advance cannot meet it all. Is it enough simply to point to the Bible miracles in the face of unbelief? Is not the Church of believers (its character, life and ministry in the newness of the Spirit's power) the world's Bible — living letters of the Holy Spirit read by all men? (2 Cor. 3:2-3). Are we not, as Christ's body, meant to be continuing His ministry both in teaching and in doing? Is it enough to talk with the compassion of Christ without being able to express it as He did in effective action, and in demonstration of the Spirit and of power? If we are able to answer "yes", we may conclude that the day of miraculous healings is past. The present writer, for one, could never give such an answer.

Appendices

APPENDIX A

The River and Tree of Life and other Allied Imagery

One of the most convincing proofs of the central place occupied by the idea of "Life" in the biblical picture of God's salvation is provided by the many symbols "of life' with which its rich imagery abounds. Besides the general ideas of "life", "long life", and "eternal life", we read of the "Spirit (or breath) of life", the "Prince of life", the "word of life", the "bread of life", the "water of life", the "book of life", the "way of life", and the "crown of life"; and from its characteristics and contents, the city of God could equally well be called the "city of life". An examination of some of these images, most of which are brought together in the Apocalypse, will confirm the picture and perspectives of life and healing in salvation which we have been attempting to expound in this book.

Some of the symbols may be passed over, as contributing little more to our general theme. Some speak of eternal life, or real life with God, with no especial reference to any particular aspect or dimension within that general concept (e.g. word, bread, book etc.), although in most cases it is made clear that we share in and enter upon this life already here and now. Some, especially the "crown of life", refer particularly to the future aspect of eternal life in glory beyond the present physical life-span (compare the "crown of righteousness", and "crown of glory" — 2 Tim. 4:8; 1 Pet. 5:4). But some of the images focus on our experience of life in this present age just as much as on any future time beyond it, and amongst these we shall especially consider the water and fountain of life (which are really the same thing, and are for drinking), the river of life (which is for irrigation and for swimming in — or paddling/wading in in the early stages!), and the tree of life, whose fruits are for eating and leaves for healing (e.g. by eating them, rubbing them on, or extracting their herbal juices). Allied to

55

these is the city of God, in which they are found (Ezek. 47;
Ps. 46; Rev. 22). In the New Testament it is made abundant-
aly clear that all these things are given to us in and through
Jesus Christ, who is "the Life", and "our life" (John 11 : 25;
14 : 6; Col. 3 : 4). For those who wish to study the various
biblical symbols of life, a list of relevant Scripture passages and verses are given at the end of this appendix. The
relevant considerations for our purposes can be briefly
summarized under four heads:

(i) The holy city of God, the new Jerusalem, in which
this river of life flows, is being built now, although it will
only be perfected and completed at the last day at the
second or final appearing of Jesus Christ, in the new
heavens and earth. It is a great misunderstanding, which
robs the people of God of many of His most precious
promises in this life, to postpone all of God's blessings except some of the so-called "spiritual" ones until either the
new heavens and earth, or some imagined future "millen-
ium"; such confusion often springs from taking the apoca-
lyptic imagery too literally, when it is plainly symbolic. The
river of God is already flowing and making glad the city of
God, and the water and fountain are to be drunk, and to
fill and flow forth from believers in Christ *now* in this
present age. And that river, water and fountain are, of
course, the Holy Spirit who is the Spirit of life Himself, and
who springs and flows to us from our Lord Jesus, who is
Life (Pss. 36 : 7-9; 46 : 4; 65 : 9; 87; John 4 : 14-15; 7 : 37-39;
Rev. 21 : 6; 22 : 17 — compare also Ps. 1 : 3; Jer. 17 : 8 *in loc.*).

(ii) The idea of life associated in Ezek. 47 : 1-12 and Rev.
22 : 1ff. with the mighty river flowing from the throne or
temple of God even now, is entirely what we should expect
from the rest of the biblical evidence. It is spiritual and
God-centred, and therefore moral or holy in its connota-
tions. But it also has its physical aspects, affecting the whole
environment. "Everything lives," in the fullest sense, "where
the river goes", human, animal and inanimate, spiritual and
physical — abundant total life.

56

(iii) That the idea of life associated with the tree and fountain of life are not simply future, and are all of a piece with the general biblical concepts of life and peace and health, can be seen from the things described as a tree, or a fountain of life in the book of Proverbs: wisdom, the teaching of the wise, the fruit of the righteous, a desire fulfilled, a gentle tongue, the mouth of the righteous etc. are all such — and many of these things are also said to bring healing and peace in the near context (Prov. 3:18; 10:11; 11:30; 13:12, 14; 14:27; 15:4; 16:22).

(iv) The tree of life is a species of tree rather than a single tree. After Gen. 2 and 3 and Proverbs (which alone speaks of "*a* tree of life") it only appears in Ezek. 47:12 and Rev. 2 and 22. It is obviously to some extent future in our enjoyment of its blessings in all their fulness, for it stands in the paradise of God, and is apparently only seen in great profusion in the new heavens and earth. Nevertheless the Ezekiel passage is surely a prediction of the experience of the Spirit in the New Covenant as a whole. Again, if it is eating from the tree of life which gives eternal life (Gen. 3:22ff.), then we must be able to eat of it now, for we already *have* eternal life (John 5:24; 1 John 5:13). Of these trees, Ezekiel states that "their fruit is for food, and their leaves are for healing", and John states that they yield varying fruit with each month, and "the leaves of the tree are for the healing of the nations". If this picture had no relevance until after the end of this age and all was to be reserved until then, we should obviously be in a difficulty. For the nations will not *need* healing in the new heavens and earth, when all are experiencing the full wholeness of God's consummated salvation. Hence plainly there is healing in the tree of life for us now.

Scripture References to some of the Main Life Images
The Tree of Life: Gen. 2:9; 3:22-24; Ezek. 47:12 compared with Rev. 22:2. "A tree of life": Prov. 3:18; 11:30; 13:12; 15:4.

The River of Life: Gen. 2:10(?); Pss. 46:4; (cf. 36:8; 65:9; also Ps. 1:3; Jer. 7:8; 31:9; Num. 24:6; Isa. 33:21; 41:18); Ezek. 47:1-12; Zech. 14:8; Rev. 22:1-2.

The Water of Life and the Fountain of Life: Ps. 36:9; Isa. 55:1; Jer. 17:13; Joel 3:18(?); John 4:14-15; 7:37-9; Rev. 7:17; 21:6; 22:17. "A fountain of life": Prov. 10:11; 13:14; 14:27; 16:22; (cf. also Isa. 12:3).

The Book of Life (*or of God, or of Jesus Christ the Lamb*):   Exod. 32:32-33; Pss. 69:28; 87:6; Isa. 4:3-4; Ezek. 9:2-6, 11; 13:9; Dan. 12:1; Luke 10:20; Phil. 4:3; Heb. 12:23; Rev. 3:5; 13:8; 17:8; 20:12, 15; 21:27.

The Crown of Life: Jas. 1:12; Rev. 2:10 (cf. 2 Tim. 4:8; 1 Pet. 5:4).

The Way of life: Prov. 5:6; 6:23; Jer. 21:8; Matt. 7:13-14; John 14:6 (*inter alia*).

The Bread of Life: John 6.

APPENDIX B

Long Life, Old Age, and the Example of Moses

At least three assessments of the longevity and aged health and strength of Moses are theoretically possible:

(a) This is meant to be a typical example of any of God's people. (b) It is meant to hold before us a possibility for faith and obedience. (c) It is only mentioned because it is so exceptional. The first view is open to question, partly because Moses was in fact one of the last of the hundred-and-tweny-year-olds, who had evidently ceased to exist by the time of the kings, and partly due to lack of consistent evidence in the Old Testament that such retention of strength was generally experienced even amongst the godly (e.g. Eli, I Sam. 4:15; David, 1 Kings 1:1ff. and Elisha, 2 Kings 13:14 etc.). The third view seems equally somewhat exaggerated in the other direction, since there are other subsequent examples in the Old Testament of godly men living to a good age and doing exploits in old age, e.g. Caleb in Josh. 14:6-15, especially vv. 10-11: "I am this day eighty-five years old. I am still as strong to this day as I was in the day that Moses sent me; my strength now is as my strength was then, for war and for going and coming" (cf. also 15:13ff.). Other examples might be cited also, as Joshua himself (Josh. 23:1-3; 24:29; Judg. 2:8).

The second view (b) therefore seems to the present writer most in keeping with the passages cited above and in the text, and is supported by other passages about longevity and senility both referring to the Old Testament era itself, and also as it looked forward to the new Messianic age. Examples of the former would be Deut. 33:25: "As thy days, so shall thy strength be", and Ps. 92:12-15, especially v. 14 "They (the righteous) still bring forth fruit in old age; they are ever full of sap and green," together with the general widespread teaching of the Old Testament that faith and righteousness bring "life and length of days" (Prov. 3:2, 16 *et. al.*). Indeed one of the main words for "health"

59

or "healing") in the Old Testament (*arūkah*) means literally a "lengthening" or "prolonging" (Isa. 58:8; Jer. 8:22 etc.). The best examples of the latter are found at the end of Isaiah (65:20), "No more shall there be in it i.e. the coming Jerusalem) an infant that lives but a few days, or an old man who does not fill out his days; for the child shall die a hundred years old . . . ." The presence of death here and other statements in the immediate context make it difficult to project the fulfilment of this passage entirely into the future beyond the return of Christ. Equally we should notice that the end of this verse, and other passages like Eccl. 6:3-6; 8:12-13, make it clear that longevity, health and temporal prosperity without the knowledge, fear and blessing of the Lord are worthless on the eternal plane.

If the view propounded above is correct, and also bearing in mind St. Paul's teaching on *phthora* ("corruption"), the question arises as to what we may expect as normal ageing in the upright believer who allows him or herself to be ruled by the love and fear of God in this life? What are the possibilities open to faith? The answer would seem to be something like this: we have no scriptural warrant for expecting or accepting "bad health" and illness from middle age onwards, but rather are encouraged to expect good health at least into the seventies as we walk with the Lord, and strength commensurate with our days. We must expect greying or whitening of the hair, weathering of the skin, and all the normal signs of ageing, but not necessarily extreme weakness and decrepitude, nor a lingering and painful illness at the end, but rather an ebbing away of life speedily at the last, as the Lord either takes the person's life and spirit quickly to be with Himself, or as the person, knowing that their hour has come to depart this life, yields up their spirit to their Creator in full consciousness and awareness of what is happening, and in peace of heart and mind. In other words, the ideal keynote is a transition in our life with the Lord, rather than a being ruled, oppressed, and tormented by death, our last enemy.

60

APPENDIX C

Job and the Problem of the Prosperity of the Wicked

(a) *Some lessons and cautions from the history of Job*[27]

Besides the observations contained in the main section of this book (pp. 19 and 24-25) — notably that health and righteousness are not always co-incidental in an individual's experience at any one moment — one or two more thoughts on the experiences of Job and the message of the book are added here, partly because it seems to be one of those sections of Scripture sometimes used to prove almost equal and opposite propositions! We simply offer these five further points for consideration.

(i) Job was himself unaware of the activity of Satan revealed to the reader in chapters 1 and 2 of the book. We should therefore beware of assuming that anyone under the New Covenant is meant to be in precisely the same position, since we are *not* supposed to be ignorant of his devices (2 Cor. 2:11), and the church has been given authority over his operations and spiritual forces in Christ's name, and gifts to discern these things (2 Cor. 10:1ff; 1 Cor. 12:10).

(ii) The book should caution us against expecting that all healing is bound to be immediate or instantaneous or obviously miraculous — it was not so in Job's case. The New Testament tells us that Job's prayer of faith and patience was heard (Jas. 5:11). A reasonable estimate of the length of Job's illness would probably be about three weeks or so, before he was healed.

(iii) If we are to be faithful to the outcome of the book, we shall have to learn with Job, therefore, to see the promises of God fufilled in the longer term sometimes, rather than just in the immediate present. We have to read chapters 1, 2 and 42 together, and compare them as a whole with the promises contained in Deut. 28 and similar passages about the Lord's blessing upon cattle, offspring etc., to the obedience of faith in His covenant. Job finished with twice as much in both kinds (family and possessions) as he had before, in the longer term. As far as his original sons and daughters who perished were concerned, it appears that they were adult, and therefore by that time responsible to God for their own souls, and we certainly have no guarantee that they were as righteous as their father (cf. Ezek. 18). Even so, their temporal deaths would not of course affect their eternal salvation either way.

(iv) The most important thing in the book from the divine or spiritual point of view is Job's reaction under trial. In one sense he is unusual, being held before us in Scripture as an outstandingly righteous man (see e.g. Ezek. 14: 13-20). His suffering, although produced by Satan, is allowed by God for a short time, because God can trust him and his reactions under it, to defeat the intentions of the enemy, and for Job to be blessed in His own character, faith and experience (or knowledge) of God. And although we ought to be very slow indeed to assume that we have been placed by God on a par with Job, and that this is the reason for our illness, nevertheless such steadfastness is enjoined upon us in trial that we may likewise grow in character and grace and knowledge of the Lord (Jas. 1 : 3ff.; Rom. 5 : 3-5). But Job's experience, and the Lord's permission of it and commendation of Job for his reaction under it, is bound to affect our notion of wholeness (especially in view of Jas. 1 : 3-4), as including development of character and spirit just as much as healing of the body.

(v) It is noteworthy that Job's reaction under physical suffering and disease gave full play to his very human emotions and feelings, which he expressed before the Lord in no uncertain manner, thus shocking his three friends. Their understanding of God's ways and promises took no account of short-term losses in order to realize longer term gains. If Job was sick, he must be a sinner, and therefore needed to confess it and repent — that was all there was to it! — and his murmurings and expression of his feelings must be given no countenance. But Job's speech, although it included wanting to die and wishing he had never been born, stopped short of cursing or renouncing God, and never ceased to affirm his faith in God's ultimate vindication of him and of his obedience in faith, even though he did not profess to understand what was going on at the time. As a result he emerges in chapter 42 as justified by his faith, as the Lord's servant (more so than his three friends), knowing God better, more assured of his prayer being heard from that time, and as one who then experiences the reality of God's promises both of healing and of prosperity. He also stands as a lasting warning to us, through the three friends, of approaching human suffering and disease with blind dogma devoid of human sympathy, humility, compassion and understanding. The present writer well remembers some years ago being visited by two different clergymen in the course of six months during a long illness. One man brought with him the text "Behold the rod and him who appointed it"; the other, who had been through the same horrible experience himself, brought the words, "What I am doing you do not know now, but you will understand hereafter." There was no doubt which visit was the greater help, nor whose words proved true.

(b) *The prosperity of the wicked — in the Psalms and other places.*

The concepts of health and prosperity belong together, in the Old Testament especially, as two parts of the concept of the peace (*shalōm*) and life which are promised to God's people in the Covenant. The Old Testament already recognizes the spiritual conflict of wickedness against the righteous, expressing itself in terms of social oppression and injustice, as well as the conflict of wickedness against God Himself. In the New Testament this becomes focussed more sharply as the spiritual conflict between the church and the world, reflecting the spiritual war to the end between Christ (the Lamb) and the angels of light and Satan (the dragon) and his forces of darkness (see Rev. *passim*; Eph. 6:10ff.;

John 15:18ff. etc.). In the longest term, the injustices resulting from the temporary continuance of evil in the world will be righted and repaid at the last Judgment. But the fact remains that many of the promises of God pertain to health and prosperity in this life here and now, and the general teaching of Scripture is that those who seek the Lord will prosper, although the Scriptures recognize that this is not invariably seen to happen; and the biblical writers do not side-step the fact that such fulfilment is not always obvious and immediate in the short term, especially to those who live in a time of declension and apostasy from God on the part of His people. (See p. 32ff. for a treatment of how this and other factors may affect our enjoyment of God's promises in this life).

One clear example of this is the prophet Jeremiah, who cries out to God,

> "Why does the way of the wicked prosper?
>
> Why do all who are treacherous thrive?" (Jer. 12:1-2)

But at the same time he makes it clear in the rest of the chapter that the prosperity of the land as a whole has been greatly reduced by the wickedness of its inhabitants. Again in chapter 5, he makes it clear that although the land is not enjoying rich harvests and regular rainfall, yet pending God's execution of judgement on the nation, wicked men by their extortion "have become great and rich; they have grown fat and sleek . . ." (5:23-31). A similar bewilderment, possibly exaggerated by his mind in his condition, is expressed by Job, who observes,

"I . . . a just and blameless man, am a laughing stock" while "The tents of robbers are at peace, and those who provoke God are secure" (Job 12:4-6). Similar and even stronger statements occur in chapter 21 of Job, but are modified and put in perspective in chapters 24 and 27. Psalms 37 and 73 are entirely devoted to the problem for faith posed to the righteous by the prosperity of the wicked. In Ps. 73, vv. 4 and 5, David mentions specifically their bodily health:

"For they have no pangs,
their bodies are sound and sleek.
They are not in trouble as other men are:
they are not stricken like other men . . . ."
A careful reading of both these psalms, however, will reveal the following factors and perspectives, which are borne out by the Bible's teaching in other places:

(i) The prosperity and health of the wicked are not universal. It is only some of the wicked who display these characteristics.

(ii) Such prosperity is short-lived, not merely in the sense that it will cease at the end of this life, which may well be sudden, but also that it frequently ceases before that (e.g. Pss. 73:17-19; 37:9-17, 34-36). Again we notice, as in the book of Job (see especially chapters 24 and 27) and in the New Testament, the need to take the longer, and not just the short-term view, remembering that God is patient and His mills grind slowly but small, and that He sees not just the individual but the family and posterity as well (Ps. 37: 28, 37-38).

(iii) Such prosperity and health are purely external and "surface", and are neither the wholeness nor the peace which are promised to those who seek the Lord and wait for Him and keep His covenant, for they do not stem from a true relationship with God in the person's spirit. The righteous may on occasion "fall, but he will not be cast headlong", for God is His stay (37:23-34). Indeed, in short-term adversity, like Job he can profit and enter into more of that wholeness of his person which the Lord want to give. And then he looks back and observes "In my prosperity I said, 'I shall never be moved' ", but "It is good for me that I was afflicted" (Pss. 30:6; 119:71 — though see v. 67 in this case). By contrast, the very "prosperity of fools shall destroy them" (Prov. 1:32).

(iv) Plainly therefore the teaching of these psalms and prophets in no way conflicts with the general teaching of the whole Bible concerning God's promises of prosperity, health and healing, for the promise of peace and prosperity to those who seek the Lord and walk in His ways is re-iterated clearly in them (e.g. Ps. 37:3-6, 11, 37-40). It may not therefore be used as an argument against our believing and appropriating the promises of God along this or any other line. But it should teach us a truer perspective in understanding His ways and purposes with men, and enable us to trust Him more surely in affliction as we lean harder upon His word, which will surely be fulfilled.

APPENDIX D

The Healings and other Miracles in the Gospels and Acts

For convenience of study and reference, a list of the healings and other miracles in Christ's ministry and in the Acts of the Apostles is given here.

Individual healings by Jesus

	Matt.	Mark	Luke	John
The nobleman's son				4:46–54
The man with an unclean spirit		1:21–28	4:31–37	
Simon's mother-in-law	8:14–15	1:29–31	4:38–39	
A leper	8:1–4	1:40–45	5:12–16	
Paralytic carried by four men	9:1–8	2:1–12	5:17–26	
Sick man at pool of Bethesda				5:2–18
The man with a withered hand	12:9–14	3:1–6	6:6–11	
The centurion's servant	8:5–13		7:2–10	
The demoniac(s) at Gadara	8:28–34	5:1–20	8:26–35	
The woman with an issue of blood	9:20–22	5:25–34	8:40–56	
Two blind men indoors	9:27–31			
Dumb man possessed with a devil	9:32–34			
Daughter of the woman of Canaan	15:21–28	7:24–30		
Deaf man with impediment in his speech		7:32–37		
Blind man at Bethsaida		8:22–26		
Epileptic boy	17:14–21	9:14–19	9:37–43	
Man born blind, sent to Siloam				9:1–14
Blind and dumb man possessed with devil	12:22–30		11:14–26	
Woman bent double for 18 years			13:10–17	
The man with dropsy			14:1–6	
The ten lepers			17:11–19	
Blind Bartimaeus	20:29–34	10:46–52	18:35–43	
Malchus's ear			22:50–51	

Healings of large numbers of people by Jesus

	Matt.	Mark	Luke	John
The crowd at Simon Peter's door	8:16–17	1:32–34	4:40–41	
Crowds, after the healing of the leper			5:14–16	

	Matt.	Mark	Luke
The crowd near Capernaum	12:15–21	3:7–12	6:17–19
Sick people healed, following John the Baptist's question	11:2–6		7:18–23
People in the crowd before the feeding of the 5,000	14:13–14		9:11
The crowd at Gennesaret next day	14:34–36	6:53–55	
People brought to Him before the feeding of the 4,000	15:19–31		
Crowds beyond Jordan	19:1–2		
The blind and the lame in the Temple	21:14		
Some sick people at Nazareth	13:53–58	6:1–6	

General statements on Christ as Healer

	Matt.	Mark	Luke	Acts
Healing all kinds of sickness and disease	4:23	1:34	4:40	
Healing every sickness and every disease	9:35			
All who touched Him were healed	14:36	6:56	6:19	
Cured those who needed healing			9:11	
Healing all who were oppressed by the devil				10:38

Christ heals through His disciples

	Matt.	Mark	Luke
Sending out of the Twelve	10:1, 7–8	6:7–13	9:1–6
Sending out of the Seventy			10:1–20

Individual healings by the disciples

	Acts
The man lame from birth	3:1–4:22
Paul regains his sight	9:10–19; 22:11–13
Aeneas the paralytic	9:32–35
The crippled man at Lystra	14:8–18
Girl with a spirit of divination	16:16–18
Paul healed of snake-bite	28:3–6
The father of Publius (fever and dysentery)	28:8

Collective healings

Many wonders and signs	2:43
In Jerusalem, many sick people healed	5:12–16

Stephen performs many miracles   6:8
Philip heals many sick people at Samaria   8:5–8
Paul and Barnabas work signs and wonders 14:3
At Ephesus, Paul heals the sick   19:11–12
At Melita, sick people healed   28:9

Other miracles in nature, grace and judgement

	Matt.	*Mark*	*Luke*	*John*
A catch of fish			5:1–11	
Calming the storm	8:23–27	4:36–41	8:22–25	
Water turned into wine				2:1–11
Feeding the 5,000	14:15–21	6:32–44	9:12–17	6:1–13
Walking on the water	14:22–23	6:45–52		6:15–21
Feeding of 4,000	15:22–39	8:1–10		
Transfiguration	17:1–9	9:2–10	9:28–36	
Coin in the fish's mouth	17:24–27			
Curtain torn and earthquake	27:51	15:41	23:45	
The catch of 153 fish				21:1–14

	Acts
Place shaken	4:31
Ananias and Sapphira struck dead	5:1–11
Angels open prison doors (and earthquake)	5:17–26; 12:6–17; 16:25–34
Saul blinded	9:3–9
Herod struck dead	12:22–23
Elymas the sorcerer struck blind	13:6–12
Paul survives the viper's bite	28:3–6

The raising of the dead (and translations)—(other than Christ's own resurrection and ascension)

Old Testament

Enoch translated	Gen. 5:24; Heb. 11:5
Elijah and the Sidonian widow's son	1 Kings 17:17–24 (cf. Heb. 11:35)
Elijah taken up into heaven	2 Kings 2:9–12
Elisha and the Shunammite woman's son	2 Kings 4:18–37 (cf. Heb. 11:35)
The man cast into Elijah's grave	2 Kings 13:20–21

Gospels	*Matt.*	*Mark*	*Luke*	*John*
The widow of Nain's son			7:11–17	
Jairus' daughter	9:18–26	5:21–43	8:40–56	
Moses and Elijah	17:3	9:4	9:30–31	
Lazarus				11:1–44
At the crucifixion	27:52–53			

Acts

Tabitha (Dorcas) raised by Peter	Acts 9:36–43
Eutychus raised by Paul	Acts 20:9–12

Footnotes

¹ G. C. Berkouwer, *Man the image of God* (Eerdmans 1962), especially chapters 7 and 8.

² Dr. Paul Tournier in *A doctor's casebook in the light of the Bible* (S.C.M. 1954) makes this point very clearly and helpfully (pp. 139ff.). Indeed, the whole of Part 3 of his book, entitled "Life, death, disease and healing", makes most interesting reading.

³ Romans 8:11 is of course a disputed text, the moot point being whether the physical quickening of the believer takes place at the resurrection (in view of the future tense), or whether it is rather in this life (in view of the "mortal" body being referred to). Neither argument is conclusive, since Pauline future tenses do not always refer to something beyond this age by any means, and since he speaks elsewhere of our *"mortality* being swallowed up by life" at the resurrection (2 Cor. 5:4). The two ideas are not necessarily mutually exclusive in any case.

⁴ This view is typically presented by T. L. Osborn in *Healing from Christ* (Osborn Evangelistic Association 1958).

⁵ E. M. B. Green, *The Meaning of Salvation* (Hodder and Stoughton 1965) pp. 218ff.

⁶ N.B. The term translated "entire" in our versions of Jas. 1:4 (*holoklēros* — meaning "whole in every part") is essentially the same word as that used in Acts 3:16 of the state of the lame beggar who had been healed, where it is well translated by A.V. (K.J.V.) as "perfect soundness" — R.S.V. has "perfect health" (*holoklēria*).

⁷ The author would not wish to deny that disease, disability etc., meekly and courageously borne and adjusted to, can and sometimes does produce refinement of Christian character under a doctrine of acceptance of these things as God's perfect will (although they can and do also produce the opposite effect). This is not, however, the point at issue here. The question is rather whether such a doctrine is actually taught by the word of God in Scripture.

⁸ See e.g. Jer. 8:14-22; 14:19; 30:12-17; 46:11.

⁹ See further G. Vos, *The teaching of Jesus concerning the Kingdom and the Church* (Eerdmans 1958), chapter 6 on "The Kingdom as the supremacy of God in the sphere of saving power", especially pp. 52ff.

¹⁰ This aspect is well presented in general terms by Anne S. White in *Healing adventure* (Arthur James, 1969) pp. 106ff., among others. See also Agnes Sanford, *The healing gifts of the Spirit* (Arthur James, 1966) pp. 100ff.

¹¹ On this, see the works of K. Koch, *Christian counselling and occultism* (Kregel, Michigan, 1965), *Between Christ and Satan* (Evangelization, W. Germany, 1967), and *Occult bondage and deliverance* (ibid., 1970).

¹² This is not a task for the novice or the uninstructed to

undertake blindly, but requires due preparation and is best undertaken by the ministers or elders of a church, or by others only in conjunction with them and under their general supervision and instruction.

13 See, however, pp. 47-48 below on the raising of the dead in this connection. K. Koch in *The revival in Indonesia* points out that the healings and miracles there took place under the immediate guidance and direction of the sovereign Holy Spirit, who instructed people as to what to do and when. It is certain that when those who exercise such ministries are hearing the Spirit's voice as clearly as this, He knows all these and any other factors which bear upon the situation and the cases and people concerned, and can therefore keep us from offering definite prayer for healing etc. when He sees the conditions not to be right, and so save us from many of the so-called "failures".

14 This is the sort of picture of St. Paul given by some of the later church historians, but is rightly described by J. B. Lightfoot in his commentary on *The Epistle to the Galatians* (MacMillan 1866) as an (admittedly fairly early) "tradition or fiction" (see pp. 183ff.). The question of the "infirmity" of 2 Cor. 12 is well handled by F. F. Bosworth in *Christ the Healer* (U.S.A. 1948) pp. 198ff., and by T. L. Osborn in *Healing the Sick* (Osborn Evangelistic Association 1959) pp. 169-180.

15 *Op. cit.* pp. 32ff.

16 As apparently by E. M. B. Green, *op. cit.* pp. 219 and 223.

17 This passage is cogently and clearly expounded along these lines by H. Horton, *Arrows of Deliverance* (A.O.G. n.d.) pp. 39ff.

18 One example of the first is in the ministry of Smith Wigglesworth — see *Faith that prevails* (Gospel Publishing House 1938) p. 23f.; the second is seen in the case of the Moslem boy Harold Khan healed in San Fernando, Trinidad, under the ministry of T. L. Osborn; the third occurred in the ministry of the Revd. R. Bolt in London in the 1960's, and was narrated to the author by those who were present. The author has also had the miraculous healings in Osborn's West Indies campaigns confirmed to him by an eyewitness.

19 I am indebted for this suggested definition to Dr. J. I. Packer of Trinity College, Bristol.

20 For a lucid treatment of this and other related questions see C. S. Lewis, *Miracles* (Fontana 1947).

21 This point is well made by K. Koch in *Between Christ and Satan* and in other works, and by Corrie Ten Boom in *Defeated enemies* (C.L.C. 1968).

22 F. L. Wyman, *The dead are raised up* (Ken-pax 1954); K. Koch, *The revival in Indonesia* (Evangelization, W. Germany, 1970) pp. 129 and 140ff.; S. H. Frodsham, *Smith Wigglesworth, apostle of faith* (A.O.G. 1949).

23 Besides the works already referred to, the reader is referred to the remarkable films, documenting the miraculous healings, made in the course of many of the Osborn crusades

around the world, including Holland (Film: *Holland wonder,* obtainable from, or viewable at, Osborn Foundation, 41 Tenby Street N., Birmingham). Also the ministry of Thomas Hicks in Argentina in 1953-4 recorded by Edward Miller in his book *Thy God reigneth* (World M.A.P. Plan 1964).

[24] B. B. Warfield, *Counterfeit miracles* (Scribner's 1918), reprinted as *Miracles yesterday and today, real and counterfeit* (Eerdmans 1954).

[25] On recently re-reading Warfield's work, one has been struck by this fact. To give but one example, his handling of the evidence around the time of Augustine (pp. 38ff.) is certainly patient of at least two other interpretations different from his own, and which would fit the evidence at least as well, if not better.

[26] Besides the review by Warfield referred to in the previous note, see also the interesting examples given in the chapters on the relevant gifts in C. J. E. Kingston, *Fulness of power* (Elim 1939; second edition 1964), especially chapter 5; and the accounts of many revivals of religion where such phenomena have undoubtedly appeared down the centuries, of which K. Koch on the Indonesian revival is only one example. For more examples of such phenomena in modern times see Jack C. Winslow, *Modern miracles* (Hodder and Stoughton 1968), and K. Kuhlman, *I believe in miracles* and *God can do it again* (Marshall, Morgan and Scott 1968 and 1970).

[27] The treatment of Job here given is in no sense meant to be complete, but only makes a number of points from that book in so far as it is relevant to our theme. For further general study see John R. W. Stott, *Why do the innocent suffer?* (Crusade reprint 1956), H. L. Ellison, *From tragedy to triumph* (Paternoster 1958), and A. B. Davidson's "Cambridge Bible" commentary on *The book of Job* (C.U.P. 1893).